Frontispiece, Picasso: *Bottle of Suze.* (1913). Pasted papers, newsprint, wallpaper, label from bottle of Suze-Apéritif Gentiane, 25¼x19⅝″. Washington University, St. Louis

the Art of Assemblage

by WILLIAM C. SEITZ

THE MUSEUM OF MODERN ART, NEW YORK

*in collaboration with The Dallas Museum for Contemporary
Arts and the San Francisco Museum of Art*

distributed by Doubleday and Company, Inc., Garden City, New York

Exhibition Dates:
The Museum of Modern Art, New York   Oct. 2 — Nov. 12, 1961
The Dallas Museum for Contemporary Arts   Jan. 9 — Feb. 11, 1962
San Francisco Museum of Art   March 5 — April 15, 1962

Library of Congress Catalogue Card Number 61-17803
© The Museum of Modern Art, 1961
11 West 53 Street, New York 19, N. Y.
Printed in the U.S.A. by the Plantin Press, New York
Color plates printed by Brüder Hartmann, West Berlin

CONTENTS

FOREWORD AND ACKNOWLEDGMENTS   6

INTRODUCTION   9

THE LIBERATION OF WORDS   13

  Stéphane Mallarmé, 13
  Guillaume Apollinaire, 14
  Filippo Tommaso Marinetti, 16
  André Gide, 17

THE LIBERATION OF OBJECTS   21

  Picasso, Braque, and Gris, 22
  Futurism, 25
  Dada and Neo-Dada, 32
  Surrealism, 39

THE COLLAGE ENVIRONMENT   72

THE REALISM AND POETRY OF ASSEMBLAGE   81

ATTITUDES AND ISSUES   87

NOTES   150

LENDERS TO THE EXHIBITION   153

CATALOGUE OF THE EXHIBITION   153

ASSEMBLAGE: A WORKING BIBLIOGRAPHY   166

INDEX   174

FOREWORD AND ACKNOWLEDGMENTS

In a press release for the retrospective exhibition of collages held at The Museum of Modern Art in 1948 Margaret Miller, director of the exhibition, wrote that "collage cannot be defined adequately as merely a technique of cutting and pasting, for its significance lies not in its technical eccentricity but in its relevance to two basic questions which have been raised by twentieth-century art: the nature of reality and the nature of painting itself. Collage has been the means through which the artist incorporates reality in the picture without imitating it." Even though the unexpected extension of the collage method that has occurred during the last few years could not have been predicted at that time, Miss Miller's comments nevertheless point out specifically its importance for contemporary art. Yet, valuable as the term "collage" remains today, the diverse works which comprise this book and exhibition call for a designation not only more embracing, but also more indicative of the mediating principles which they demonstrate.

Save for a few calculated examples, the physical characteristics that these collages, objects, and constructions have in common can be stated simply:

1 They are predominantly *assembled* rather than painted, drawn, modeled, or carved.
2 Entirely or in part, their constituent elements are preformed natural or manufactured materials, objects, or fragments not intended as art materials.

If it were not typographically awkward, the title of this book could have been "The Art, Non-Art, and Anti-Art of Assemblage," for, though the painterly collages of Esteban Vicente or the welded constructions of David Smith and Ettore Colla approach painting or sculpture, and though a majority of the works included are unquestionably works of art, others were fabricated expressly to dispel an aura of authority, profundity, and sanctity. Some, such as the wittily speculative objects of Man Ray, were "designed to amuse, annoy, bewilder, mystify, inspire reflection but not arouse admiration for any technical excellence usually sought or valued in objects classified as works of art."[1] There are even some pieces here that cannot be called "art" at all in the accepted sense of that term. They are "readymade" assemblages: portions removed from the everyday environment without alteration, and presented "on a plane apparently not suited to them"[2] for a special kind of examination.

Neither the exhibition nor the book is a detailed survey, either of the technique of collage and its expanded forms, or of the movements within which these innovations occurred. If anything has been surveyed, it is the metaphysics of assemblage rather than its history. To the degree that both the text and the exhibition are — inevitably, I feel — historical, they attempt to follow one among the many threads that lead through the labyrinth of twentieth-century styles. The walls of its compartments are not immovable; each added viewpoint changes their arrangement.

To bring together works, some of them controversial, by little-known as well as well-known and famous artists entails many evaluations, reconsiderations and anguishing exclusions. I owe a special debt of gratitude, therefore, to those who, in the United States and in Europe, gave assistance, information, and suggestions that led to the final selection. Especially to be mentioned are: Lawrence Alloway, Irving Blum, Pieter Brattinga, Mr. and Mrs. William N. Copley, Bruce Conner, Daniel Cordier, Richard Hamilton, Walter Hopps, Dr. K. G. Hultén, Ivan Karp, Jean Larcade, Kynaston L. McShine, Dr. Dietrich Mahlow, Miss Georges Marci, Morton G. Neumann, Mrs. John Rewald, the Misses Niki and Elizabeth de Saint-Phalle, Arthur Schwarz, Eberhard Seel, Joseph R. Shapiro, Miss Odyssia Skouras, Jean Tinguely, Dr. Herta Wescher, and Mme Edith Zerlaut-Rauscher.

I wish to thank others for specific services: the critics, artists, and publishers who permitted the quotation of relevant material, in some cases unpublished; Kate Steinitz and William Cartwright for assistance in studying the Watts Towers, and, for his fine color photographs of them, Seymour Rosen; Bernard Karpel, not only for his scholarly bibliography, but also for his pioneer "research in image" for assemblage, still in progress; Irene Gordon, who criticized the manuscript in both typescript and galley proof; Alicia Legg for, along with other assistance, preparing the catalogue; Frances Pernas, for her skill and devotion in the production of the book; and Lucy Lippard for preparing the index. Extra hours given by other colleagues must also be recognized.

For special assistance, I wish to thank Paul Kantor, Leo Castelli, Mr. and Mrs. Michael Sonnabend, Eugene Thaw, and Mr. and Mrs. William H. Weintraub.

On behalf of the Trustees of The Museum of Modern Art, The Dallas Museum for Contemporary Arts, and the San Francisco Museum of Art I also extend my gratitude to the collectors, museums, dealers, and artists listed on page 153, whose loans have made the exhibition possible.

WILLIAM C. SEITZ, *Associate Curator*
Department of Painting and Sculpture Exhibitions

Picasso: *Still Life with Chair Caning.* (1911-12). Oil and pasted oil cloth simulating chair caning, oval, 10⅝x13¾″, with rope around edge. Owned by the artist

INTRODUCTION

In May 1912, Picasso finished a small oval still life into which was pasted a fragment of oil cloth that simulated chair caning and around which, in lieu of a frame, he wrapped a length of hemp rope. This cubist composition seems abstract at first glance, but after a short study of the intersecting lines and translucent planes some of its elements can be identified. The letters J O U , which float ambiguously from their position in space toward the surface of the picture, are plainly remnants of the word "Journal," and make up an abbreviated representation of a newspaper. The profiles of a sliced lemon and a glass can be recognized, and at the upper left, above the letters, the stem of a pipe seems to project forward into the actual space in front of the picture. Somewhat less clearly, a knife, and what could be a shell, can also be detected. Common objects of the café table, human in scale, they are those that the fingers manipulate idly, and often unconsciously.

Such subject matter, characteristic of cubist painting, reminds one that the arrangement of ordinary objects, from ancient times until those of the Dutch still-life painters, Chardin, Manet, Fantin-Latour, Harnett, Cézanne, and Picasso, is a form of preliminary assembled art. Moreover, the placement, juxtaposition, and removal of objects within the space immediately accessible to exploration by eye and hand is an activity with which every person's life is filled, virtually from birth until death.

Violating the limitations of representation, the *Still Life with Chair Caning*, in which "Picasso juggles reality and abstraction in two media and at four different levels or ratios,"[3] initiates the absorption of the activity of assembling objects into the method, as well as the subject matter, of painting. Everyone familiar with modern art knows that the area representing a caned surface, and seemingly painted in a *trompe-l'oeil* technique, is in fact an actual fragment of commercially printed oil cloth. Because of the second innovation, the rope frame, the entire composition is forced into the

Spoerri: *The Pail Is Not Arman's*. 1961. Household utensils glued to wooden board, 17¼x47″. Galleria Schwarz, Milan

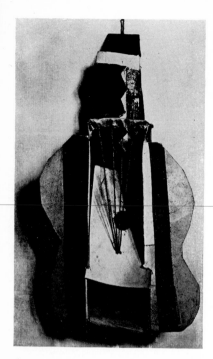

Picasso: *Guitar*. 1912. Construction of colored papers and string, 13x6¾″. Owned by the artist. Reproduced from Zervos, *Picasso*, vol. 2, pt. 2, pl. 770

world of objects, like a nautical plaque or a table finished at its periphery with a spiral molding. It could even be said that this "recklessly adulterated"[4] work, which (at least as far as the main stream of modern art is concerned) began the development of collage,[5] also initiated three-dimensional assemblage; Picasso's colored-paper *Guitar* was constructed during the same year, 1912, and the *Mandolin*, described by Alfred Barr in 1935 as "neither sculpture nor painting, nor architecture,"[6] was put together two years later from scraps of discarded wood.

Every work of art is an incarnation: an investment of matter with spirit. The term "assemblage"[7] has been singled out, with this duality in mind, to denote not only a specific technical procedure and form used in the literary and musical, as well as the plastic, arts, but also a complex of attitudes and ideas. Just as the introduction of oil painting in fifteenth-century Flanders and Italy paralleled a new desire to reproduce the appearance of the visible world, collage and related modes of construction manifest a predisposition that is characteristically modern.

The sensibility responsible for, and at the same time formed by, modern art — among its creators were Baudelaire, Guys, Manet, and Rimbaud — is often ironic, perverse, anti-rational, and even destructive. Yet, with its negative side fully recognized, this temperament is one of the beauties that has flowered in the dark soil of twentieth-century life. It is worthwhile to follow the paths and consider the modes by which the modern artist's sensitized and irritable personality developed, for the methods and metaphysics of collage have similar origins and patterns of growth. Together, modern art and modern personality form a development that is neither a suite of isolated compartments nor a purely temporal sequence. Rather it expands in streams, interconnected pools, and eddies, like a complex river system.

In looking backward at the early masterpieces of cubism one is struck almost as sharply by their connection with the past as by their modernism. Judged not only by more recent innovations and by the pace of other events that occurred while they were being painted, but also by the nineteenth-century substratum of relationalism that preceded them, they seem conservative rather than radical by now. The compression of form and space toward two-dimensionality was already implicit in Ingres' *Odalisques*, and an emphasis on juxtaposition was clearly apparent by 1865 in the paintings of Whistler and Manet. Manet's quasi-academic and sophisticated early compositions — from the *Absinthe Drinker* of 1859 to the *Luncheon in the Studio* ten years later — hide behind their dissembling surfaces, eclecticism, and aestheticism an ironic, anti-rational relativism that does not become overtly apparent until the time of Apollinaire, Satie, and Duchamp.[8]

In spirit if not in technique, Manet can also be seen as a precursor of the collagist. His famous portrait of Emile Zola includes a pin-up board like that found today in almost every artist's studio. Affixed to it, a photograph of Manet's *Olympia*, a print by Utamaro, and Goya's etching after Velázquez' *Los Borrachos* form an overlapping "collage" of the disparate elements that Manet's art incorporated.[9] On the table below, a decorated inkwell and its feathered quill, soft yellow, pink, and blue paper books, and other objects have been arranged with far more regard for color and pattern than for accessory significance. The printed signature MANET — calling to mind the use of lettering in the *papiers collés* of Picasso and Braque — can be read as the title of the book at the right. Indeed, if Manet's first line of development had not

Edouard Manet: *Portrait of Emile Zola*, 1868, detail.
Musée du Louvre, Paris

been deflected by the new trend epitomized by Monet, he might have evolved a two-dimensional art that would have been a foretaste of Matisse in form, with a "dada" irony (which runs like a dye through Manet's art) as a content.

The advent of impressionism postponed realization of these potentialities for, although Monet's "series" pictures of the 1890s were composed of a multitude of competing particles of color, the roseate mists in which these touches all but coalesce approached homogeneity. Monet wished to translate a momentary and cohesive perceptual response into pigment. But Cézanne, who utilized impressionism for his profound dislocation of Poussinist solidity, irreversibly undermined accepted modes of representation and coherence. If it was Manet who placed the *banderillas* in the body of the Renaissance tradition, it was Cézanne who (with a much less subversive intent) drove the blade toward its vitals. The hills, mountains, and rocks in his landscapes shift as in an earthquake; the earth's surface bends and splits from his heroic attempt to reconcile classical art with conflicting data of feeling, perception, and structural intuition.

The scale and profundity of this awesome disturbance of the established geology of Western art is most accessible in his still lifes. All but disassembled, and perceptually deformed, the fruit, bottles, and dishes attract and repel each other within a pictorial constellation that art had never seen: each element is altered through what Roger Fry called "a strange complicity between these objects"[10] as if by a mutual recogni-

Haberle: *The Changes of Time*. 1888. Oil and gesso on canvas mounted on masonite, 23¾x15¾". Collection Marvin Preston, West Ferndale, Michigan

tion — what Whitehead termed "prehension" — of each for the other. In figure compositions arms, legs, torsos, and even heads shorten, stretch, or twist under the pressures of Cézanne's pondered readjustments. Caught between a love of the past and a commitment to the future, he struggled with the problem of relating parts and aspects to the wholes that they compose — articulating an embracing change in realization that found its most illuminating explanation in Gestalt psychology.[11]

Also within this ambiance, Seurat conceived art as a harmony of "contrary and of similar elements."[12] He pioneered in establishing an abstract aesthetic of multiple confrontation — of the horizontal to the vertical, of light to dark, of rising to falling movements, and of the "simultaneous contrast" of warm and cool colors. The rules he applied were later reworked by Delaunay and the futurists, and form the basis of the philosophical and formal principles empirically evolved by Mondrian. Seurat's pointillist systemization of impressionist technique, which resulted in a surface of beveled facets,[13] began the redivision of Monet's perceptual unity. In accord with a host of other related influences, the relativism evidenced by Cézanne and Seurat offered to the artists of what Apollinaire called "the new spirit" the syntax for a sharp break with previous modes of aesthetic coherence.

THE LIBERATION OF WORDS

It is difficult for minds nurtured by skepticism, materialism, and pragmatism to grant the existence of immaterial realities; yet it is not difficult to demonstrate that the climate of ideas out of which the technique of collage arose existed independently of the many media in which it took form. It was the poets, working with less physical and more immediately responsive materials than the painters and sculptors, who, cherubim and seraphim fluttering in celestial light, responded most rapidly and directly to the spirit of the times. Futurism and dada began as literary and political, rather than plastic, movements; surrealism originated in the automatic literary technique practiced by Apollinaire, the first spokesman for cubist painting; his poetry, that of Max Jacob, Blaise Cendrars, and Pierre Reverdy, and certain of the novels of André Gide, have been called "literary cubism."

The arrangement of words, each carrying with it "an image or an idea surrounded by a vague aura of associations,"[14] is close to the method of collage. The poet's most important tool is the metaphor — "the joining of two things which are different."[15]

STÉPHANE MALLARMÉ

It was the poetry of Mallarmé, poised in a fragile balance at the meeting point of impressionism and symbolism with "the new spirit," that suggested the confrontation of fragments as a literary method. The *White Water Lily* of 1885, like the music of Debussy, is impressionistic and symbolistic; but the crucial *Un Coup de dés jamais n'abolira le hasard* of 1897 postulates another aesthetic not only in its radical topographical arrangement and its emphasis on the idea of chance, but also in its pattern of images and its projection toward a "pure" poetry resembling music or abstract painting. The title is a sentence cut into fragments that are distributed, as four topical headings, through the poem: "A throw of the dice — never — will abolish — chance."

Without rhyme or meter, and with individual words or word-groups arranged in patterns, the poem evolves like a cinema — "a kind of intellectual film" — in which "every page should be considered in its entirety, as though it were a picture."[16] Roger Fry (who understood so well the relational dynamite of Cézanne's still life) points out how, in looking intently at ordinary objects, Mallarmé also anticipated cubist still life: "No one has given to the words for common objects so rich a poetical vibration — fenêtre, vitre, console, verrerie, pierrerie, lampe, plafond — and this by no forced note of admiration or willed ecstasy, but by an exact observation and deduction of their poetical implications."[17] With Mallarmé, Fry goes on to say, the theme is "frequently as it were broken to pieces in the process of poetical analysis, and is reconstructed, not according to the relations of experience but of pure poetical necessity."[18]

But to dub Mallarmé a "cubist" poet is to distort his historical position. He surely pushed the traditional modes of thematic development and continuity almost to their breaking point but, as Roger Shattuck has explained in a lucid paragraph, not beyond it: "Juxtaposition in modern literature began where Mallarmé stopped. He reached a point from which any advance must abandon the possibility of *meaning* in the classical sense."[19]

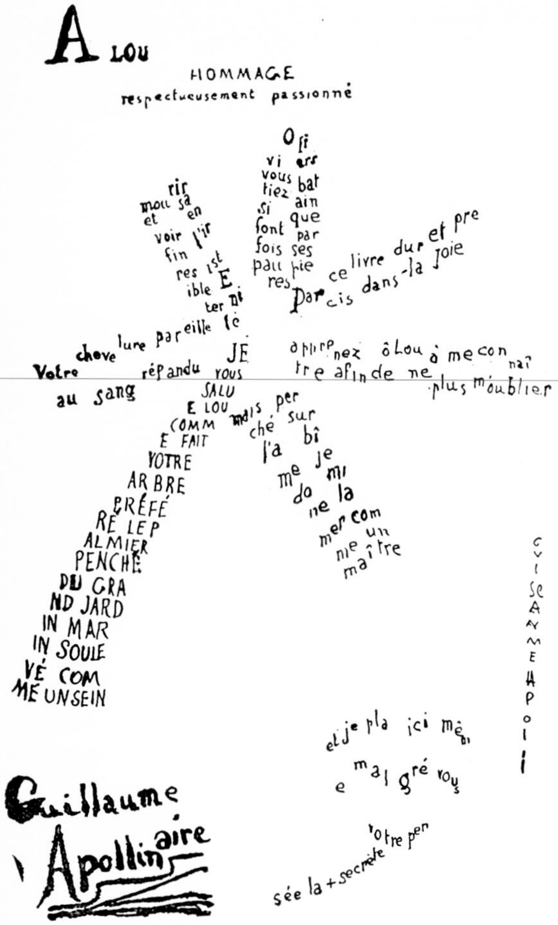

A LOU

HOMMAGE
respectueusement passionné

O si
vi ers
vous bat
tiez ain
si que
font pàr
fois ses
pau tie
res

rir
nou sa
et en
voir l'ir
fin ist
res ist
ible E
ter ni

Dar cis dans -la joie
ce livre dur et pre

chove lure pareille le
Votre
au sang répandu vous JE apprenez ô Lou à me con nai
SALU tre afin de ne plus m'oublier
E LOU
COMM mais per ché sur
E FAIT j'a bi
VOTRE me je
ARBRE do mi
GREFFÉ ne la
RE LE P mer com
AL MIER nie un
PENCHE ma ître
DU GRA
ND JARD
IN MAR
IN SOULE
VÉ COM
ME UN SEIN

GUILLAUME APOLLINAIRI

et je pla ici mê
e mal gré vous

votre pen
sée la + secrète

Guillaume Apollinaire

Guillaume Apollinaire: Reproduced from *Oeuvres Poétiques, Poèmes à Lou, II*, Paris, *Nouvelles Revues Françaises*, 1956, p. 378

GUILLAUME APOLLINAIRE

Guillaume Apollinaire was the first of the twentieth-century figures — Marcel Duchamp and André Breton were two others — who served as accumulators of avant-garde ideas. Prophet and merchandiser as well as poet, he was both seismograph and tuning fork, simultaneously absorbing and propagating vibrations that ranged from symbolism, cubism, and futurism to dada, surrealism, and abstract art. His defense of collage and *papiers collés* in *The Cubist Painters*, published in 1913, far surpasses in boldness the cubist painting of that year: "You may paint with whatever material you please, with pipes, postage stamps, postcards or playing cards, candelabra, pieces of oil cloth, collars, painted paper, newspapers." He cites the use of blood as a painting medium by someone during the French Revolution, and mentions an Italian artist who painted with excrement.[20]

In poems as early as 1908, Apollinaire had moved "toward freedom in assembling a poem out of disparate parts."[21] During 1912, the year of the first *papiers collés*, Apollinaire spoke of a new source of inspiration: "prospectuses . . . catalogues, posters, advertisements of all sorts. Believe me, they contain the poetry of our epoch. I shall make it spring forth."[22] Apollinaire, the spearhead of diverse cross influences — among them the *simultanéisme* of Delaunay, the new medium of the film,[23] the futurist proclamations of Marinetti, and cubist collage — along with Salmon, Max Jacob, Cendrars, and other cubist poets, decided to use as poetical material any words or word combinations, however mundane, jarring, or disassociated they might appear. In Apollinaire's simultaneist and "orphic" poems, ideograms, and "calligrams," separate parts are allowed more autonomy than are analogous elements in the cubist *papiers collés* of the time. Snatches of conversation, routine phrases, and clichés follow one after the other without transition or thematic connection:

> *Trois becs de gaz allumés*
> *La patronne est poitrinaire*
> *Quand tu auras fini nous jouerons une partie de jacquet*
> *Un chef d'orchestre qui a mal à la gorge*
> *Quand tu viendras à Tunis je ie ferai fumer du Kief*
>
> *Ça a l'air de rimer*

From Lundi Rue Christine[24]

Apollinaire combined the method of juxtaposition (often visually as well as poetically) with an appropriation of the verbal environment: he implicitly posed, that is to say, the principles of an art assembled of actual, rather than verbal, objects. Georges Duhamel's criticism of *Alcools* (a book of Apollinaire's poems published in 1913) makes this apparent:

> Nothing could remind one more of an old junk shop than these collected poems. . . . I call it an old junk shop because a mass of heterogeneous objects has found a place there and, though some of them are of value, none of them has been made by the dealer himself. That is just the characteristic of this sort of industry: it resells, but it does not produce. Sometimes there are strange objects for sale; on its grimy shelves one may discover a rare stone hanging from a nail. All this comes from afar, but the stone is pleasant to look at. The rest is a collection of faked paintings, patched exotic garments, bicycle accessories and articles of intimate hygiene. A truculent and bewildering variety takes the place of art in this assemblage. . . .[25]

The "calligrammatic" style, which came closer to painting than Picasso and Braque's *papiers collés* did to poetry, was defined by Apollinaire himself in his magazine *Soirées de Paris*. The principle underlying collage could not be explained more aptly:

> *Psychologically* it is of no importance that this visible image be composed of fragments of spoken language, for the bond between these fragments is no longer the logic of grammar but an ideographic logic culminating in an order of spatial disposition totally opposed to discursive juxtaposition.
>
> . . . It is the opposite of narration, narration is of all literary forms the one which most requires discursive logic.[26]

FILIPPO TOMMASO MARINETTI

The rebellious "new spirit" trumpeted by Apollinaire was not parochial. His ideas were as colored by futurism as they were by cubism. The initial manifesto of futurism was published in Paris. Apollinaire (born in Rome and interested in all things Italian) was acquainted with its author, the poet Filippo Tommaso Marinetti, and wrote an article on futurist painting in *Mercure de France* in 1911, almost before futurist theory had taken form in painting. Marinetti's idea of "words at liberty," put forward in his manifesto on literature published in May 1912,[27] is a frontal attack on syntax. It calls for the abolition of punctuation, of the adjective and adverb, and of all traditional devices that qualify and give rational continuity to word images. The verb is to be used only in the infinitive, and the noun is to be followed by another noun associated with it only intuitively, by sound, or by free association. Anticipating dada and surrealism, Marinetti denounced all scientific or "photographic" categories; prophetic of dada, also, was his willingness to accept any image whether noble or base, elegant or vulgar, eccentric or normal, that upset the despised classical hierarchy of ideas and values.

Marinetti's typographical "collages," such as *A Tumultuous Assembly*, go much further than either Apollinaire or the cubists in eliminating the distinction between

Filippo Tommaso Marinetti: *A Tumultuous Assembly* (*Une assemblée tumultueuse: sensibilité numerique*). From F. T. Marinetti, *Les mots en liberté futuristes*, 1919, p. 109

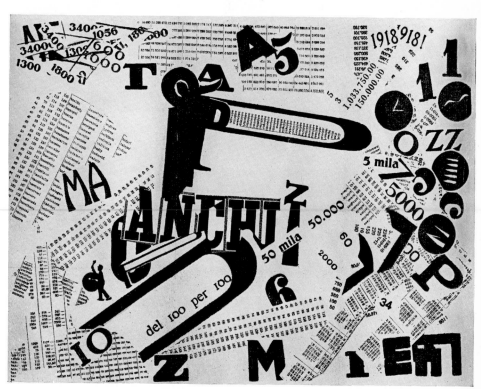

literary and visual arrangement. In one jump, Marinetti crossed the threshold at which, moving in the opposite direction, collagists were beginning to usurp the prerogatives of poetry. It can be said of both Marinetti and Apollinaire, however, that, more than two years before the dadas, they had sanctioned the separation of the word from punctuation, rhyme, meter, narration, and thematic continuity, stopping just short of dada accidentalism and the psychic automatism practiced by André Breton and the surrealist painters.

ANDRÉ GIDE

Before 1914, while Braque, Picasso, and Gris were assembling their first collages, André Gide was writing his "cubist" novel *Lafcadio's Adventures* (*Les Caves du Vatican*). As in certain drawings of Jean Cocteau or Saul Steinberg, representation of the subject is caught up short by an intruding image of the artificer's hand at work, but Gide's relativism is more encompassing than that of the cubist painters. Lafcadio, a free man committed to a gratuitous, unmotivated act, moves, like Marcel Duchamp's "Sad Young Man in a Train," through a sociological landscape of ambiguously shifting morality and immorality, truth and falsehood, Freemasonry and Catholicism by which ethical and social opposites are confounded and neutralized.

For *The Counterfeiters* (*Les Faux-Monnayeurs*, 1925), Gide worked out a method, intentionally dispersive, from his earlier attack on the structure of the novel. He replaced traditional narration by a coreless sequence of events and data strung together almost without common theme: "The difficulty arises from the fact that I must start anew with each chapter," he tells himself while writing *The Counterfeiters:* "*Never take advantage of momentum* — such is the rule of my game."[28] To the extent that a "plot" can be said to exist in this novel, it is made explicit only in the loosely connected acts of the protagonists, presented piecemeal in several manners and from divergent viewpoints: through snatches of conversation, correspondence, journal entries, newspaper articles, and unresolved speculations by an author who, like his readers, is at the end left quite unsure of the denouement. In its recurrent speculation on reality and artificiality, *The Counterfeiters* is cubist: "But I thought you wanted to abandon reality," the (fictional) author is queried. "My novelist wants to abandon it; but I shall continually bring him back to it. In fact that will be the subject; the struggle between the facts presented by reality and the ideal reality."[29] "Gide's art," as Wylie Sypher writes, "has the excitement of interruption, of fracture."[30] By disassociation, by refusing to resolve disparate elements, he retains an openness more typical of life than of art.

Additional examples of the aesthetic of juxtaposition are easy to find in literature, not only among the writings of cubism, dada, or surrealism, but also in the work of Eliot, Joyce, Pound, Cummings, Marianne Moore, Ionesco, and other writers whose modernism corresponds to that of contemporary painting and sculpture. Examples quite as enlightening can also be drawn from the music of composers such as von Webern, Satie, Varèse, or John Cage; and exact parallels to plastic assemblage exist in taped *musique concrète*. The assembler is especially akin to the modern poet, however, in using elements which (unlike "pure" colors, lines, planes, or musical tones) retain marks of their previous form and history. Like words, they are associationally alive.

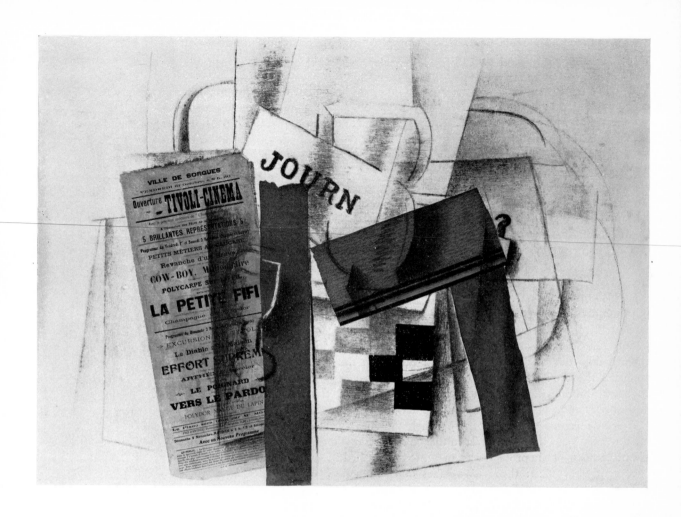

Picasso: *Still Life with a Calling Card*. (1914).
Pasted papers and crayon, 5½x8¼″. Collection
Mrs. Gilbert W. Chapman, New York

opposite, Braque: *The Program*. (1913). Pasted papers, charcoal, and oil on canvas, 25⅝x36¼″. Collection Mr. and Mrs. Bernard J. Reis, New York

Braque: *Clarinet*. (1913). Pasted papers, newsprint, charcoal, chalk, and oil on canvas, 37½x47⅜″. Collection Nelson A. Rockefeller, New York

Gris: *Breakfast*. (1914). Pasted paper, crayon, and oil on canvas, 31⅞x23½″. The Museum of Modern Art, New York. Acquired through the Lillie P. Bliss Bequest

Picasso: *Still Life*. (1914). Painted wood and upholstery fringe, 10x18⅞". Collection Roland Penrose, London

THE LIBERATION OF OBJECTS

L'objet réel ou en trompe-l'oeil est appelé sans doute à jouer un rôle de plus en plus important.
Il est le cadre intérieur du tableau et en marque les limites profondes, de même que le cadre
en marque les limites extérieures.
GUILLAUME APOLLINAIRE[31]

Art should never be valued according to the speed with which it rushes toward some hypothetical future. The slow, stage-by-stage evolution of cubist form between 1908 and 1915, in fact, may be a measure of the greatness of its artists. Daniel-Henry Kahnweiler described cubism as the reconciliation of a conflict between representation and structure.[32] Cézanne had canonized the willful deformation and fragmentation of objects and human figures, and had provided the authority to supplant "pictorial composition" by another kind of structural order. Conservative in their choice of subject matter, the cubists nevertheless adapted it to their formal ends willfully and even capriciously.

"Each epoch always has and always needs its oppositions of destruction and construction," Piet Mondrian wrote.[33] Modern art and the modern sensibility have developed through a rhythm of metaphoric destructions and reconstructions. It could be said, for example, that the "analytical" phase of cubism (about 1909-1912) constituted — to use a less ominous term than "destruction" — a "disassemblage" of the world of represented objects, each work dismantling a selected aspect of the environment to provide raw material for a structured image with a metaphoric rather than an imitative reference to the world. The cubist transformation of reality, accomplished in successive plastic statements, is surely as important a background to the method of assemblage as is the recourse to pasting: cubist collage was as much an outcome as a deviation or a cause. From conservative themes, cubist painters and sculptors constructed a new order that pointed directly toward abstract art. Their compositions of generalized fragments were compressed into a space that (compared, let us say, to the space of Poussin or Caravaggio) was gradually flattened like the closing of a bellows. Ambiguous, faceted, and shallow, it gave form to a new set of principles demonstrable in music and literature as well as in painting and sculpture.

PICASSO, BRAQUE, AND GRIS

Picasso and Braque said little, in words, of their battle with illusionism from 1909 to 1911; yet picture by picture — even passage by passage and stroke by stroke — the phases of its dialectic are stated. Perhaps unintentionally, they appropriated the tangibility of impressionist brushwork in order to pack their foregrounds with evocative, but ultimately irreducible, facets. Using a repertoire of brilliant (and in the case of Picasso, at least, ironic) innovations they played back and forth between recession behind the canvas surface and projection forward from it. Gradually, they limited the deep space by which artists had represented the world since the fifteenth century. The objects they depicted no longer diminished in size or disappeared in light and atmosphere. Immediate and tangible, their subjects were pressed forward by the advancing rear wall of the picture, so that cubism became an art of the close-up, that dealt with what was, literally as well as figuratively, "close at hand." " . . . by its very subject matter," Kahnweiler wrote, "it has made us 'see' and love so many simple, unassuming objects which hitherto escaped our eyes (kitchen and household utensils, musical instruments, etc.)."[34]

    Picasso, Braque, and Gris all indicated, at one time or another, a distaste for the slickness of oil paint.[35] With the illusionistically painted nail that appears to be hammered into the surface of Braque's *Still Life with Violin and Pitcher* of 1909-10, the sweeping adulteration of media we are witnessing today was already prefigured.[36] When, in the interplay between fiction and fact, objects formerly within the picture space appeared, at one-to-one scale, on its surface, when the picture plane offered a support on which letters, numbers, and words could be stenciled without distortion, the advent of collage was all but inevitable. Soon a label could be pasted on a picture as appropriately as on a bottle (frontispiece), or a calling card left "in" a picture as naturally as on a table (page 18). "You want to know why I had to stick on a piece of mirror?" Gris later said to Michel Leiris: "Well, surfaces can be re-created and volumes interpreted in a picture, but what is one to do about a mirror whose surface is always changing and which should reflect even the spectator? There is nothing else to do but stick on a real piece."[37] Because Gris' seemingly realistic images were arrived at deductively, from arrangements of geometric forms, because his art was more self-consciously philosophical, and because he explained his method, the use of collage is less problematical in his work than it is in that of Picasso and

Laurens: *Seated Woman.* (1918). Cut and pasted cardboard, with charcoal, 39x26½″. Collection Mr. and Mrs. G. David Thompson, Pittsburgh

Braque. For him, Kahnweiler asserts, it was only a means of getting real details, of abolishing "tricks of brushwork and of replacing the 'hand-painted' surface by the 'ready-made.' "[38] Interpolations of non-art materials provided an "internal frame" — a fragment of actuality erupting within a fictional environment. They violated the separateness of the work of art, and threatened to obliterate the aesthetic distance between it and the spectator.

It would be absurd to suggest that the shift from oil painting to Marcel Duchamp's "readymades," (pages 46-47), Rauschenberg's "combine-paintings," (pages 116-117), or the untouched *décollage* of the *afficheurs* (pages 82, 108-109) could have been extrapolated on the basis of Picasso's *Still Life with Chair Caning;* yet it must be conceded that, by the introduction of a bit of oil cloth and a length of rope, the sacrosanctness of the oil medium suffered a blow that was as deadly as it was deft, and that the three-dimensional constructions by Picasso, Tatlin, and others who followed challenged the accepted criteria of sculpture even more overtly. According to Kahnweiler, Picasso wished to "debunk the idea of 'noble means,' " and thus romantically and ironically to "display the pre-eminence of the creator's personality over his creation."[39] But at the same time, Kahnweiler saw in *papiers collés* (especially those of Gris) a deliberate

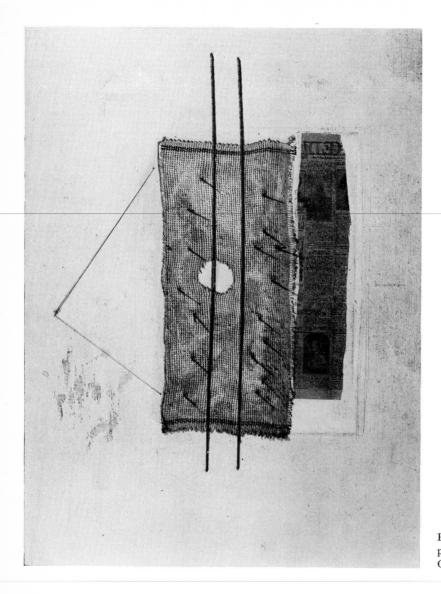

Picasso: *Guitar*. 1926. Sackcloth with string, pasted paper, oil paint, and cloth pierced by two-inch nails, 51¼x38¼". Owned by the artist

gesture toward impersonal authorship; he notes that between 1908 and 1914 Picasso and Braque usually signed works only on the reverse side, and that Gris followed that practice in 1913 and 1914.[40]

As a corollary to these retrospective speculations, one should not forget the importance of the cubist reassembly of the environment for the beginnings of abstract painting and sculpture. Nearly every work of assemblage, in its relational structure, approaches abstract art; but it is worth noting that — unlike Delaunay, Kupka, Malevich, Lissitzky, Kandinsky, or Mondrian — Braque and Picasso never painted pure abstractions. Both of them retained their identification with objects. In its employment of "live" materials, therefore, assembled art continues the realism of cubism as well as its relativism. Parallel with the "cubist" novels of Gide, which made a break with narration, and music that abandoned melody and accumulative themes, cubism rejected perspective, chiaroscuro, and atmospheric color. But communication with the past was never cut off; the separation, so to speak, never became a divorce, either in the willingness to discard realism entirely for abstraction, or to dispense with thematic coherence.

In cubist paintings, moreover, and often in collages as well, the ambiguously beautiful device of *passage* — a final attempt to soften the shock of discontinuity — tends to bridge disassociations of image. The method of assemblage, which is post-cubist, is that of *juxtaposition:* "setting one thing beside the other without connective."[41]

It is of course impossible to place the ruthlessly inventive genius of Picasso within any theoretical framework. By 1914 his assemblages (such as *Still Life*, page 21) anticipated those of Schwitters and Miró, and the immediacy of the rough sackcloth and the dangerously projecting nail-points in *Guitar* (1926), despite its cubist image, points toward an even newer aesthetic. His recent three-dimensional assemblages, which he has cast in bronze, are as youthfully iconoclastic as a work by any artist under thirty.

Although in its structure assemblage is like abstract painting and constructivist sculpture, it diverges sharply from these traditions not only because its raw elements are associationally "charged," preformed, and often precisely identifiable (nails, photographs, old letters, weathered wood, automobile parts, leaves, doll's eyes, stones, or whatever), but also because its ultimate configurations are so often less predetermined. Futurism's "beautiful Ideas that kill"[42] and the nihilism of dada were a necessary preparation. Like abstract art, however, the most characteristic assemblage occupies real space. Physically, its method can be as direct as filling a cupboard or setting a dinner table. Herein lies one outcome of cubism's dialectic between illusion and actuality: formerly, the space and form of painting was physically false, and that of sculpture physically real. Cubism closed the painted picture-window to make of it the painting-object: a part of the environment that projects quite naturally into three dimensions. Questioned in Paris as to why he added objects to his paintings, Robert Rauschenberg answered: "Paint itself is an object, and canvas also. In my opinion, the void which must be filled does not exist."[43]

FUTURISM

The contribution of Italian futurism to the aesthetic of assemblage is not limited to Marinetti's liberation of words. Apollinaire's prophetic proclamation on the unrestricted use of unorthodox materials was preceded by Boccioni's assertion, in the *Technical Manifesto of Futurist Sculpture* of April 11, 1912, that "a Futurist composition in sculpture will use metal or wood planes for an object ... furry spherical forms for hair, semicircles of glass for a vase, wire and screen for an atmospheric plane, etc." In the next paragraph he affirms "that even twenty different materials can compete in a single work to effect plastic emotion. Let us enumerate some: glass, wood, cardboard, iron, cement, horsehair, leather, cloth, mirrors, electric lights, etc., etc."[44]

It seems more to be expected that Italy, rather than France, would have extended art media by extraneous materials, for Italy is the land of gesso painting, tooled gold halos, ex-votos, the preservation of relics, inlaid marble, intarsia, and mosaic. In 1899 the painter Mancini exhibited a canvas in Venice in which the metallic keys of a clarinet were imbedded in a painted representation of it; he also imbedded bits of glass, tin foil, and other foreign substances to obtain rich textural effects in his paint surface.[45] Severini's use of materials such as sequins began after a conversation with Apollinaire concerning the use of objects in Italian fifteenth-century paintings such as Crivelli's *Madonna and Child with Four Saints* in the Brera Gallery in Milan, in which Saint Peter carries a solid replica of a large gold key hanging on a real cord.[46]

At the international exhibitions of modern art held in April 1914 in Rome and in London, the "object sculptures" by Balla, Marinetti, and Cangiullo were given much attention; Balla experimented in impermanent materials, as did Boccioni. Most of these works are lost, but examples of true assemblages by Boccioni and Marinetti have been documented in photographs. Boccioni's *Fusion of a Head and a Window* (page 28), which included a real wooden window frame and fastener, was done in 1911 or perhaps 1912, the year of the first collages of Picasso and Braque.[47]

But, radical though these prefigurations were, it cannot be said that words, materials, and objects were given full freedom in futurist collage. Futurism was a movement in which social and aesthetic theory preceded the practice of painters and sculptors. Its works were the carriers of a passionately felt and explicit subject matter — nationalism, war, the speed of automobiles and airplanes, the sublimating power of light, psychological interpenetration with the environment, etc. — that exerted an even tighter control over form than did the unspectacular motifs of cubism. Although certain futurist principles such as "innate complementariness" and "simultaneity" seem to posit confrontation, they in fact relate to the ideas of Delaunay (or even of German expressionism) more than they do to those of Picasso or Braque. At least in part, futurism was an extension of urban impressionism and neoimpressionism rather than an opposition to them; and the emphasis on kinetic continuity and simultaneity led to repeated overlapping, and transparent images that interpenetrated and blended. Projecting "lines of force" were used to suggest speed, continuity, and the fusion of objects with their environment. A painter was enjoined not merely to paint the figure, but to "render the whole of its surrounding atmosphere,"[48] and the materiality of masses was intentionally dissolved in light and superimposition, by cultivating a vision "giving results analogous to those of the X rays."[49] Stroboscopic multiplication of images led to blending rather than maintenance of interval. In their most sublime aspirations, the futurists proclaimed themselves "Lords of Light," who "drink from the live founts of the sun."[50] Unlike cubists their aims could not therefore lead to a close-up examination of textures, materials, or objects; futurism's key words are "interpenetration" and "synthesis" rather than "interval" and "juxtaposition." This being the case, it should not be surprising that the collages of Severini, who worked in France, most resemble those of Picasso and Braque; that the fragment of newsprint in Boccioni's *Cavalry Charge* (page 30) serves to identify the battle which is the picture's subject; or that, in Carrà's warlike free-word collage *Patriotic Celebration*, typography is whirled in a centrifugal vortex that confounds a propaganda message with a dizzying spiral of inciting fragments, sounds, and colors.

Carrà: *Patriotic Celebration*. (1914). Pasted papers and newsprint on cloth, mounted on wood, 15¼x12″. Collection Dr. Gianni Mattioli, Milan

Boccioni: *Fusion of a Head and a Window.* (1911). Plaster and wood. (Sculpture destroyed.) Reproduced from Carrieri, *Avant-Garde Painting and Sculpture in Italy*, Milan, Domus, 1955

Severini: *Still Life with Cherries*. (1913). Pasted papers, newsprint, oil, etc., 19½x26½". Collection Mr. and Mrs. Harry Lewis Winston, Birmingham, Michigan

Umberto Boccioni: *The Cavalry Charge.* (1915). Tempera, pasted papers, and newsprint on cardboard, 12⅞x19½″. Collection Dr. Riccardo Jucker, Milan

Although the futurist movement has had far fewer followers of either its formal principles or its ideological program than has cubism, its importance for later art, in both form and spirit, has been immense. It should be recognized that, in the fury of its struggle to displace the stultifying weight of past styles, its eagerness to confront the most brutal and sublime realities of the present and the future, and its high-keyed concern for "a completely renovated sensitiveness,"[51] futurism spoke prophetically for most avant-garde movements. Periods of nihilism are, as Mondrian realized, as necessary for the continued vitality of the arts as are periods in which the past is revered and emulated. The futurists succeeded in placing the dynamic world of steel, glass, and speed at the center of art while rebelling against the tyranny of Ancient and Renaissance authority, "harmony," and "good taste." Their endeavor to break the strictures imposed by socially approved forms and attitudes, in order to enter "at any price" into life, was carried on after the decline of futurism by the dadas, who were pacifistic and internationally minded rather than nationalistic and war-like.

Malevich: *Lady at the Advertising Pillar*. 1914. Oil on canvas, with pasted papers, lace, 28x25¼″. Stedelijk Museum, Amsterdam

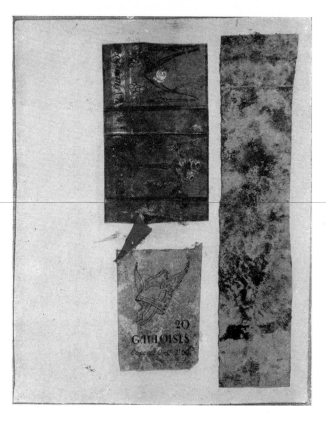

Stella: *Collage No. 7.* (ca. 1921). Pasted papers and cardboard, 11x8⅞". Zabriskie Gallery, New York

Picabia: *Les Centimètres.* (1918). Oil on canvas, with centimeter tape, matches, etc., 21½x14¾". Galleria Schwarz, Milan

DADA AND NEO-DADA

The recent wave of assemblage, which has disturbed supporters of both figurative and abstract art, has repeatedly been designated, often in disdain, as "neo-dada," even though its manifestations are far too varied to be so categorized. Moreover "dada" — as it should no longer be necessary to reiterate — was not, like futurism, a cohesive movement. Astringent but meaningless, the term "dada" was applied to an unpremeditated international eruption of feeling that had already begun. "The more we contemplate," Richard Huelsenbeck writes in his *Dada Manifesto 1949*, "the more evident it becomes that the creative principle developed in Dadaism is identical with the principle of modern art. Dadaism and modern art are one in their essential presuppositions."[52] On the other hand, the ideas put forward during the dada period can be found not only in assemblage and "junk culture" but also in abstract expressionism and other current work. Willem de Kooning spoke of Duchamp in 1951 as "a

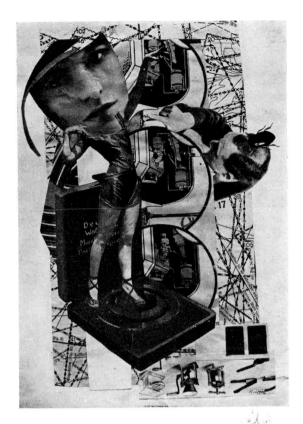

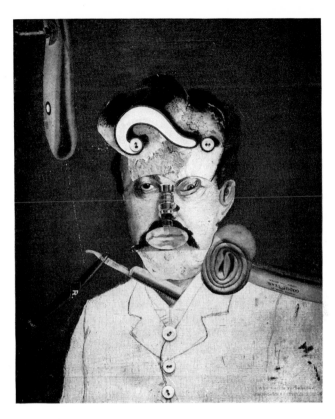

Höch: *Collage*. (1920). Cut and pasted illustrations, 14x11⅞″. Collection Mr. and Mrs. Morton G. Neumann, Chicago

Grosz: *"Remember Uncle August, the unhappy inventor."* 1919. Oil on canvas, with charcoal, magazine advertisements, buttons, 19¼x 15⅝″. Collection Mr. and Mrs. Bernard J. Reis, New York

one-man movement," but "a movement for each person and open for everybody."[53] Yet, the admixture of dada in assemblage must not simply be granted; it must be insisted upon, and if possible, understood.

During the period in Zurich before the movement was christened in 1916, dada was, as Huelsenbeck has repeatedly explained, a nameless antiwar and literary manifestation with an aesthetic commitment to abstract art. Sociologically, international dada was the response of bitter and spiritually injured intellectuals to a war and postwar atmosphere that was distasteful to them — the reverse of futurist jingoism. Dada's targets, however, were not too different from those of futurism: entrenched authority, cultural and social stupidity and hypocrisy, pedantry, and the utilization of past art as a dead hand with which to stifle experience. Whether in the United States, Switzerland, France, or Germany, dada propagated ideas and attitudes abhorrent to the complacent bourgeois mind: tomfoolery, accident, irrationality, use of vulgar language, symbolic vandalism, and contempt for venerated cultural standards.

Judged by a morality that places a high value on tranquillity, certain dada activities were surely pernicious. Year by year, however, the positive and elevating contributions of the dada artists and poets to modern thought are becoming more evident. Partly by intention — but surely at first without understanding what they were about — the dadas and their marvelously pungent creations and activities raised a mirror in which the absurdities of the social world were reflected. By ridicule and inversion, dada demonstrated that the true determinants of many ritualized public acts and professed social goals are fortuitous or base.

In its contacts with the public, whether in the raucous incidents that occurred in New York, Zurich, Hanover, Cologne, Berlin, Paris, or Barcelona, or in the collages, photomontages, "readymades," and other art, anti-art, and non-art objects that

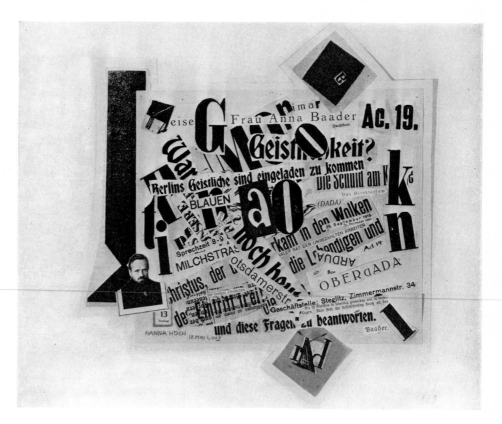

Baader: *Commemorative Leaf for Gutenberg.* 1919. Pasted printed material with photograph of the artist, 13⅞x19⅞". Collection Frau Hannah Höch, Berlin

Arp: *Collage with Squares Arranged According to the Law of Chance*. (1916-17). Pasted papers, 19⅛x13⅝″. The Museum of Modern Art, New York. Purchase

they fabricated, the method of the dadas was shock; their immediate intent was con-fusion — the desire to make the spectators also dadas by inciting their indignation. They brought to a sharp focus the dilemma in which choice between alternatives was impossible. "What is beautiful? What is ugly? What is great, strong, weak?. . . What is 'I'?" Georges Ribemont-Dessaignes asked, and answered "Don't know! Don't know, don't know, don't know!"[54] Tristan Tzara, in his *Dada Manifesto 1918*, sees opposites as equivalent: "Order=disorder; ego=non-ego; affirmation=negation."[55]

Of all dada's varied contributions to practical — that is to say nonacademic or nonprofessional — philosophy, and through it to the theory and practice of the arts, the most important (for it encompasses all the others, even the celebration of individ-ual freedom) was its attention to negative values. Not only did this apparent perverse-ness cast a merciless light on meretricious public morality; it discovered beauty and worth in what was commonly held to be distasteful and valueless.

Hausmann: *Mechanical Head*. (1918). Wood, metal, leather, cardboard, 12¾″ high. Collection Frau Hannah Höch, Berlin

opposite, Arp: *La Trousse du voyageur*. (1920). Wood construction, 7⅝x13″. Collection Tristan Tzara, Paris

Unsureness and confusion, in the arena of dada opinion, became a positive value, one that had lethal effect on systems of hierarchy and classification. In the spirit of Jarry, dada postulated a "pataphysical" logic of absurdity within which Marcel Duchamp could establish a syntax (recalling Marinetti's poetic method) based on similarity of sound rather than meaning.

For a study of the attitudes by which modern art has been activated, the terms "cubism," "futurism," and "dada" should denote an interrelated sequence of currents. They point to a period in which brilliant and daring, if sometimes irresponsible, minds totally fragmented or altered traditional and even advanced modes. Perhaps even more important: finally and with authority — and for the first time in Western thought — dada substituted a nonrational metaphysic of oppositions for a rationalized hierarchy of values. As a consequence it accorded to unsureness, accident, confusion, disunity, and discontinuity a share of the attention formerly reserved for what had been commonly regarded as their moral opposites, and released a constellation of physical and intellectual energies through which an artist could (and still can) operate in a way that, at least in the West, was previously impossible. By a dynamism inherent in human experience, moreover, the recognition of live reciprocity turns the mind toward an indefinable central principle as transparent and vital as the Tao in Chinese thought and art. It was the knowledge of dada, in part, which led certain modern artists, after 1945, toward Zen Buddhism.

It is hard to overemphasize the deep mark made by the ironic and anarchic temper

Baargeld: *The Red King*. 1920. Pen and ink on pasted wallpaper, 19⅜x15¼″. The Museum of Modern Art, New York. Purchase

Ernst: *The Chinese Nightingale*. (ca. 1920). Pasted photographs and halftones, 4¾x3⅜″. Collection Tristan Tzara, Paris

which, with roots in eighteenth-century skepticism, was incorporated into the culture of painting by Guys, Baudelaire, and Manet, and came to a brawling yet mystical climax in dada. The method of assemblage is inconceivable without dada's negativism, for the precondition of juxtaposition is a state of total randomness and disassociation. Like a beachcomber, a collector, or a scavenger wandering among ruins, the assembler discovers order as well as materials by accident. At the start at least, his is an atmosphere without conditions, an alternating current in which hierarchies of great and small, order and disorder, good and bad, beautiful and ugly, are reversible or nonexistent. Physically, his raw material is the random assemblage of the modern world in which nature and man are thrown together in an often tragic and ludicrous, but fertile and dynamic, disarray: the crowded city, the split-level suburb, the "moon shot," the picture magazine, the summit conference, the television western. Dada awakened senses and sensibilities to the immense multiple collision of values, forms, and effects among which we live, and to the dialectic of creation and destruction, affirmation and negation, by which life and art progress.

Quite properly, dada liquidated itself before its creations entered the museums. By now, the masterful collages and constructions of Schwitters, the enigmatic works of Duchamp, the masterpieces of Jean Arp, and miscellaneous dada innovations by poets, composers, film makers, and typographers as well as painters and sculptors have gained official sanction along with other twentieth-century tendencies. Over and over history makes it clear that (at least by a sociological definition) the appellation "work of art" is a blue ribbon awarded to certain chosen activities and artifacts that, as defined by a given climate of opinion, are felt to have enriched human existence.

Considered solely as a liberating creative method, dada offered (and still offers) a dispersive context within which untried kinds and degrees of organization could (and still can) arise from a state of randomness and disorder. In the most thoroughgoing sense its process differs from that of realism, expressionism, or even surrealism. As Tristan Tzara emphasized in 1953, dada sweepingly affirmed the principle, previously proposed by Apollinaire and the futurists, that art could be created by any elements whatsoever: "materials noble or looked down upon, verbal clichés or clichés of old magazines, bromides, publicity slogans, refuse, etc. — these incongruous elements are transformed into an unexpected, homogeneous cohesion as soon as they take place in a newly created ensemble."[56] The type of unity that results from juxtaposition, however, can never be entirely preordained, for an assembled work grows by testing, rejection, and acceptance. The artist must cede a measure of his control, and hence of his ego, to the materials and what transpires between them, placing himself partially in the role of discoverer or spectator as well as that of originator. Although this method can be adapted to very different attitudes, and incorporated in very different technical processes, it begins, in its essence, with elements that are dispersed and diverse. Indeed, by a paradox crucial to the understanding of modern art, dispersion and disruption can even be inseparable from cohesion and unity. Physically and metaphysically, assemblage is the ultimate outcome of the mode of juxtaposition initiated before 1900.

SURREALISM

The central principle of surrealism, as André Breton defined it in his manifesto of 1924, was its recourse to "pure psychic automatism." Whether employed as a means of introversion (as it is by Dali, Magritte, and other "photographic" surrealists) or as a technical procedure (which it became for Masson, Miró, Matta, Gorky, and, finally and most completely, for Jackson Pollock), automatism differs from the accidental method of dada, or the relationalism of abstract art. Breton found in Lautréamont, Rimbaud, and Mallarmé "a real *insulation*, thanks to which the mind, on finding itself ideally withdrawn from everything, can begin to occupy itself with its own life...."[57] Automatic expression, which moves outward from the center of consciousness, is continuous, viscous, and biomorphic. Assemblage is its opposite; for it originates in unrelated fragments and, like realism or even impressionism, draws from the environment. Yet, as a corollary to introversion and automatism, surrealism retained the method of juxtaposition.

In analyzing the psychology of surrealism, Marcel Jean speaks of the "pulsation" of conscious and unconscious, centripetal and centrifugal forces.[58] He also demonstrates the juxtapositional orientation of the great early work of de Chirico. "From 1914-15 onwards," Jean writes, "assemblages of objects become the centre of interest: gloves, hands from anatomical models, eye-glasses, cigar boxes, etc. . . . compositions resembling still-lives in the open air. . . ."[59] The connection of these dreamlike confrontations to the real environment is apparent in de Chirico's reminiscence of an urban image, from his early days in Paris: "The huge glove in painted zinc, with its terrible golden finger-nails, swinging over the shop door in the sad wind blowing on city afternoons, revealed to me, with its index finger pointing down at the flagstones of the pavement, the hidden signs of a new melancholy. . . ."[60] With de Chirico as with Henri Rousseau, a disquieting beauty results from "an unexpected juxtaposition between objects which are in themselves banal."[61] De Chirico, as James Thrall Soby writes, had a "genius for poetic dislocation."[62]

The surrealists drew the idea of juxtaposition, dazzlingly epitomized in the now-famous "convulsive" image of the "chance encounter of a sewing machine and an umbrella on a dissecting table,"[63] from Lautréamont as well as de Chirico. "This unexpected, arbitrary beauty, these dumbfounding juxtapositions are the very voice of Surrealism," Georges Hugnet wrote for Alfred Barr's *Fantastic Art, Dada, Surrealism*.[64] Max Ernst derived his definition of both surrealism and collage from Lautréamont's metaphor. Collage, as defined by Ernst, is an exploration of "the fortuitous encounter upon a non-suitable plane of two mutually distant realities."[65] Super-reality (in a citation of Breton by Ernst) is "a function of our will to put everything completely out of place."[66] Ernst explains in detail how, by juxtaposing ordinary but — reversing cubism's thematic conformity — *unrelated* entities in a situa-

Exquisite Corpse (collaborative drawing). Copy after a lost original by André Breton, Greta Knutson, Valentine Hugo, Tristan Tzara (ca. 1933). Ink, 9½x12″. Collection Mr. and Mrs. Morton G. Neumann, Chicago

Ernst: Collage of photoengravings. From the collage novel, *Une Semaine de Bonté*, Book I, 1934

tion where neither belongs, poetic transformation will result. Here, reduced to its simplest terms, is the principle underlying surrealist collages, assembled objects, and the collaborative drawings known as exquisite corpses.

No painter's work ever embraced a wider range of inherent contradictions than that of Max Ernst. The most divergent poles of intellectual position, style, and technique, ranging from geometric abstraction to microscopic realism and from careful planning to *frottage* and automatism, stand side by side, often in the same work, with jolting arbitrariness. In one among his many manners — and it is one of his strengths that they are irreconcilable — he is the collage painter par excellence. The collages of the dada period, pasted together from fragments of technical, anatomical, and other illustrations, are assemblages in every sense, as were his objects. In later work, however, especially in the collage "novels" such as *Une Semaine de Bonté*, the physical identity and discreteness of the original segments is intentionally lost in a new synthetic representation. As in the paintings of Magritte — whose unnerving images brilliantly exemplify the surrealist principle of juxtaposition — these collages retain irrational confrontations on a representational plane but, having become homogeneous erotic or oneiric illustrations, they have relinquished the physical and structural basis of collage.

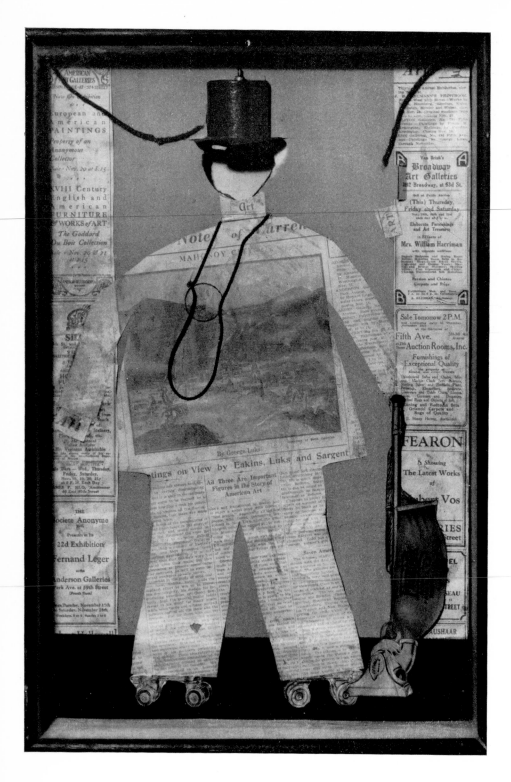

Dove: *Grandmother*. (1925). Shingles, needlepoint, page from the Concordance, pressed flowers, 20x21¼". The Museum of Modern Art, New York. Gift of Philip L. Goodwin

opposite, Dove: *The Critic*. 1925. Newspaper clippings, magazine advertisements, velvet, etc., on cardboard, 19x12½". The Downtown Gallery, New York

Duchamp: *Fresh Widow*. 1920. Miniature French window with leather-covered panes, 30½x17⅝". The Museum of Modern Art, New York. Katherine S. Dreier Bequest

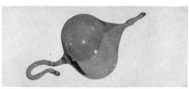

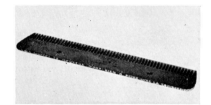

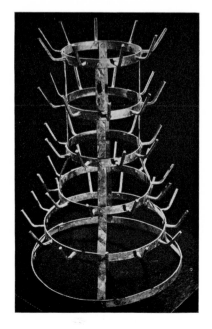

Readymades by Marcel Duchamp; left, top to bottom: *With Hidden Noise* (1916), *Paris Air* 1919, *Comb* 1916, *Bottle Dryer* 1914; right, top to bottom: *Why Not Sneeze?* 1921, *Fountain* 1917. See also *Bicycle Wheel* 1913, opposite.

For additional data see exhibition catalogue, page 158.

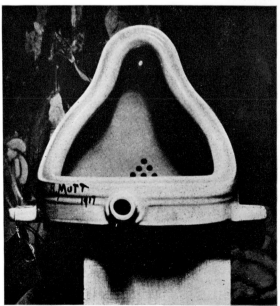

47

Man Ray: *Theatr.* 1916. Pasted paper and newsprint with crayon, 18x24″. Galerie Rive Droite, Paris

In whatever form it is finally presented: by a painting, by a photograph, by an arrangement of various objects, or by one object itself slightly modified, each object is designed to amuse, annoy, bewilder, mystify, inspire reflection but not to arouse admiration for any technical excellence usually sought or valued in objects classified as works of art.

There has been a tendency in the past fifty years to extend the boundaries of legitimate art; in painting by the use of materials extraneous to canvas and pigment, in sculpture by the employment of other materials than the classic bronze or stone that identify such sculpture as a work of art. Of course, many have remained faithful to the traditional materials for fear that their authenticity as works of art might be questioned, at the same time forcing their medium into new paths and utilizing it in as unacademic a manner as possible. To attain this end, it has been necessary to resort to new sources of inspiration such as primitive art, the works of the insane and of children, the dream world, black magic, mathematics, and logically uncontrolled, or automatic impulses. However, the human interest in a basic order and logic, governed by pre-established rules remains intact. The surprises that may occur within such limits are sufficiently exciting to most men. There is also a security in this interest not to be found in the uncertainties and diversity of opinions that are involved in art appreciation. Which leads to such activities as stamp or butterfly collecting, chess playing, and sports in general of a competitive nature. These more or less scientific interests justify themselves by precise measures of value and excellence based on comparisons or numbers, just as in school our proficiency is indicated by graduated ratings. Now, we all love a mystery, but very few of us would be content with a mystery for its own sake, that is without a solution. Little does it matter that, once the solution is obtained, we go on to another mystery, or once a champion has proven himself, by however slight the margin, that he must still defend his title.

Between these two domains of art and play, another spirit exists

which seeks neither the authority of consecrated art, nor the justification of any effort in work or play of a competitive nature. It is a sort of gratuitous invention, an establishment of mystery inspired by and responding immediately to the contacts that might be ignored by specialists and professionals. Whatever form of expression this spirit may take, since it cannot easily be classified among the more recognized activities, one cannot approach it with the usual critical bias. In assembling "Objects of My Affection," the author indulged in an activity parallel to his painting and photography, an activity which he hopes will elude criticism and evaluation. These objects are a mystery to himself as much as they might be to others, and he hopes they will always remain so. That is their justification, if any is needed.

"We all love a mystery, but must it necessarily be murder?"

MAN RAY
Preface from a proposed book,
One Hundred Objects of My Affection

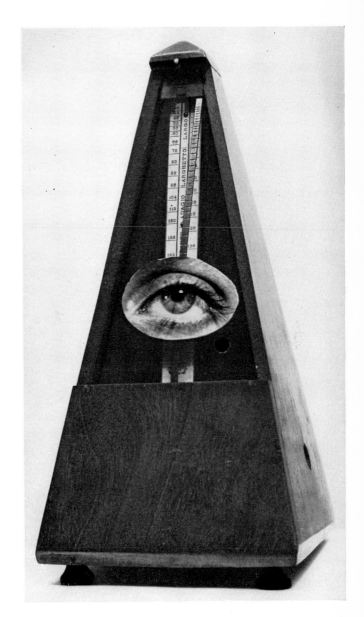

Man Ray: *Indestructible Object.* (Replica of the earlier *Object to be Destroyed*). 1958. Metronome with cutout photograph of eye on pendulum, 9″ high. Collection Mr. and Mrs. Morton G. Neumann, Chicago

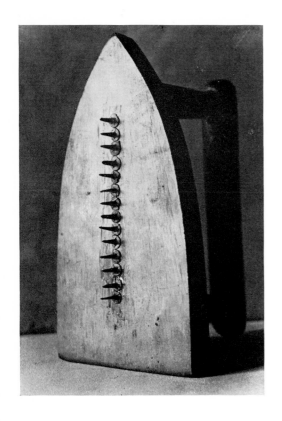

left, Man Ray: *Le Cadeau.* Flat iron with metal tacks, 6½″ high. Collection Mr. and Mrs. Morton G. Neumann, Chicago

49

It now seems to me that even striving for expression in a work of art is harmful to art. Art is an archprinciple, as sublime as the godhead, as inexplicable as life, undefinable and without purpose. The work of art is created by an artistic evaluation of its elements. I know only how I do it; I know only my material, from which I derive, to what end I know not.

KURT SCHWITTERS
Translated from "Merz," Der Ararat, 2, Munich, Goltzverlag, 1921, p. 5.

Schwitters occupies a position of special honor in the history of assemblage, for his ideas and works prefigure even the most recent developments. It was he who conceived of an embracing medium that included painting, collage, agglomerate sculpture, theater, architecture, typography, poetry, and even a form of singing. An Anna Blume (To Eve Blossom) is his most successful poem, but the most important is Die Sonate in Urlauten (Sonata in Primitive Sounds), inspired by Raoul Hausmann's sound-poem fmsbw, which Schwitters heard in 1921. He worked on this abstract recitative refining it through repeated performances, until about 1928, and it was published in 1932 in Schwitters' MERZ magazine.

MERZ was the name given by Schwitters to his new universal medium. The word was taken from the title of a collage in which he had incorporated a fragment from an advertisement for the Kommerz und Privatbank. There are about twenty large MERZ pictures, hundreds of smaller ones, and innumerable MERZ drawings (which are in fact small collages). Three MERZ architectural constructions were his most ambitious undertakings. The first Merzbau, built in Schwitters' home in Hanover and called the Column, or Cathedral of Erotic Misery, was the only one completed. In its final state it became an abstract construction, but when seen by Kate Steinitz about 1924, "rising from a chaotic heap of varied materials," it was a "three-dimensional collage of wood, cardboard, iron scraps, broken furniture and picture frames." It had "not only formal, but also expressive significance through literary and symbolistic allusions. The Column was a depository of Schwitters' own problems, a cathedral built not only around his erotic misery, but around all joy and misery of his life and time. There were cave-like openings hidden in the abstract structure, with secret doors of colored blocks. These secret doors were opened only to initiated friends. There was a Murderer's Cave, with a broken plaster cast of a female nude, stained bloody with lipstick or paint; there was a caricature abode of the Nibelungen

Detail of Schwitters' *Merzbau* in his home at Waldhausenstrasse 5, Hanover, Germany, ca. 1924 (later covered by a more abstract structure). Includes Schwitters' pet guinea pig

in miniature; in one of the caves a small bottle of urine was solemnly displayed."[69]

The Hanover Merzbau was destroyed by bombs in 1943. Later Schwitters began a second such construction in Lysaker, near Oslo, Norway, which was destroyed by fire in 1951. Portions of a third, begun in a barn in Ambleside, England, are still in existence.

Detail of Schwitters' *Merzbau*, ca. 1933. For additional details see *Fantastic Art, Dada, Surrealism*, The Museum of Modern Art, 1936, figs. 670, 671

opposite, Schwitters: *Cherry Picture*. 1921. Pasted papers, etc., 36⅛x27¾″.
The Museum of Modern Art, New York. Mr. and Mrs. A. Atwater Kent, Jr. Fund

Schwitters: *Merz Drawing (Merzzeichnung)*. 1924. Pasted papers
and a button, 7¾x6⅛″. The Museum of Modern Art, New
York. Katherine S. Dreier Bequest

Schwitters: *Drawing 6 (Zeichnung 6)*. 1918. Pasted papers, etc.,
7x5½″. Collection Mr. and Mrs. Solomon Ethe, New York

Schwitters: *Merz 25: A Painting with Stars*. 1920. Oil and collage. Private collection, Lysaker, Norway

opposite, Schwitters: *Merz Construction*. (1921). Wood, wire mesh, paper, cardboard, etc., 14½x8½″. Philadelphia Museum of Art, Philadelphia, A. E. Gallatin Collection

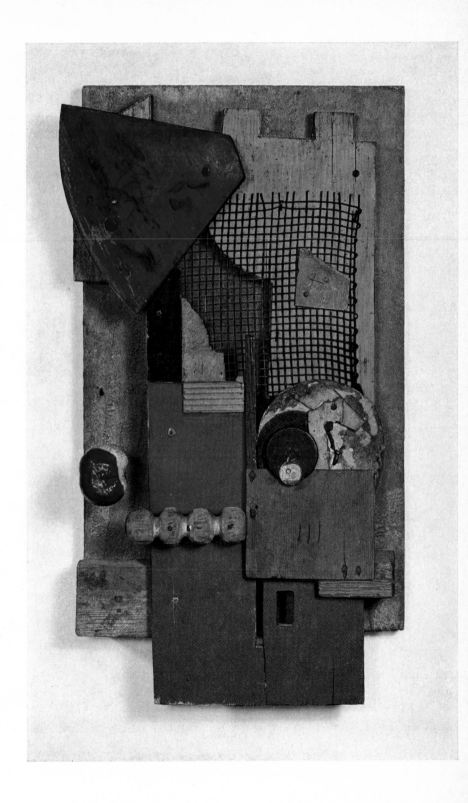

Schwitters: "*Yes — What?*" ("*Ya — Was Ist?*"). 1920. Oil, pasted papers, corrugated cardboard, cloth, nail heads, wood, 38½x27¼". Collection Mr. and Mrs. James W. Alsdorf, Winnetka, Illinois

Schwitters: *The Neatest Trick of the Month.* (ca. 1943-45). Pasted papers, photograph, etc., 16¾x21″. Collection Richard S. Zeisler, New York

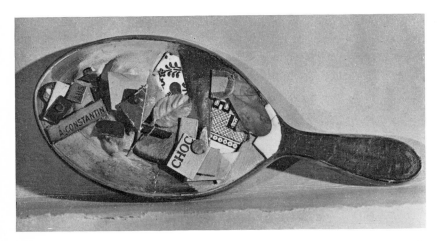

Schwitters: Untitled. (1920). Oil, pasted papers, etc., on hand mirror, 12½x8⅞″. Collection Tristan Tzara, Paris

Mannequins shown in the International Exhibition of
Surrealism, Galerie Beaux-Arts, Paris, January 1938.
Left: Salvador Dali; right: Wolfgang Paalen

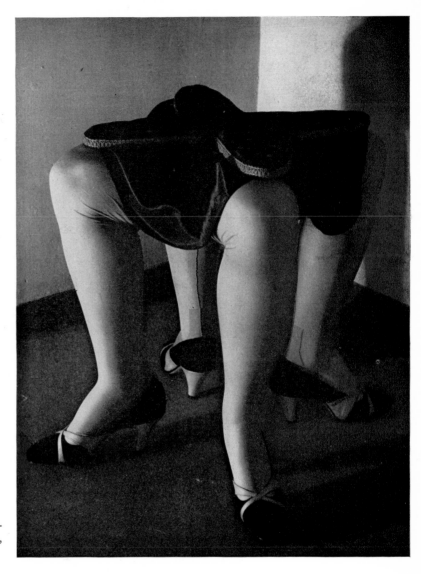

Kurt Seligmann: *Ultrameuble*. Shown in the International-al Exhibition of Surrealism, Galerie Beaux-Arts, Paris, 1938. Destroyed in hurricane, Sugar Loaf, N. Y., 1949

I was determined to carry out and transform into reality my slogan of the "surrealist object" — the irrational object, the object with a symbolic function — which I set up against narrated dreams, automatic writing, etc. . . . And to achieve this I decided to create the fashion of surrealist objects. The surrealist object is one that is absolutely useless from the practical and rational point of view, *created wholly for the purpose of materializing in a fetishistic way, with the maximum of tangible reality, ideas and fantasies having a delirious character.*

SALVADOR DALI
from The Secret Life of Salvador Dali,
New York, Dial, 1942, p. 312

left, Vail: *Bottle*. Painted bottle and stopper, encrusted with plaster, cork, sponge, feathers, etc., 16¾″ high. Collection Mr. and Mrs. Bernard J. Reis, New York; center, Vail: *Bottle*. 1947. Painted bottle, with pasted papers, spectacles, etc., 16″ high. Galerie Iris Clert, Paris; right, Magritte: *Bottle*. Painted bottle with carved wood stopper, 12″ high. Collection Mr. and Mrs. Joseph R. Shapiro, Oak Park, Illinois

Bryen: *Objet à fonctionnement: "Morphologie du désir."* (1934-37). Mounted casts of ears; wood, candle, flashlight, plywood, 7⅞″ high x 14½″ wide x 11″ deep. Owned by the artist

opposite: left, Oppenheim: *Squirrel.* (1960). Glass beer mug, plastic foam, fur, 8⅝″ high. Galleria Schwarz, Milan; right, Oppenheim: *Object.* (1936). Fur-covered cup, saucer, and spoon. The Museum of Modern Art, New York. Study Collection

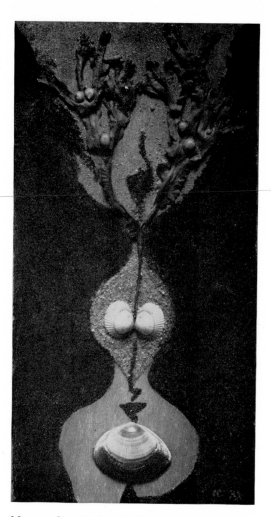

Miró: *Composition Collage*. 1933. Pasted papers, sandpaper, with gouache, charcoal, pencil and ink, 42½x28″. Collection Royal S. Marks, New York

Masson: *Caryatid*. (1939). Tempera, sand, seaweed, seashells, on wood, 13¾x7⅛″. Galerie Louise Leiris, Paris

opposite, Miró: *Objet poétique*. (1936). Stuffed parrot, wood, man's hat, and other objects, 33¼″ high. Pierre Matisse Gallery, New York

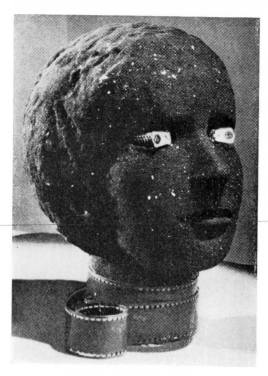

Jean: *Spectre of the Gardenia*. 1936. Plaster, covered with black cloth; zippers, movie film, 10½″ high. Owned by the artist

Brauner: *Wolf-Table*. 1939. Wood with parts of stuffed animal, 21⅝″ high x 22⅞″ long x 11″ wide. Owned by the artist

Miró: *Object.* (1932). Painted stone, shell, wood, and mirror-glass on wooden board, 22″ long x 9¾″ wide. Philadelphia Museum of Art, A. E. Gallatin Collection

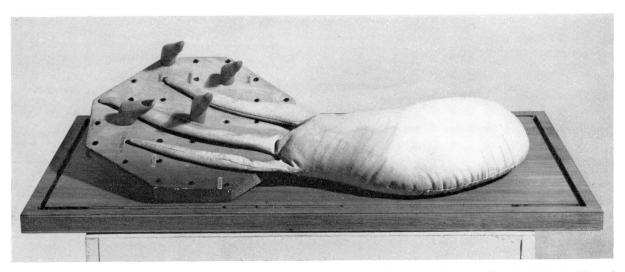

Tanguy: *From the other side of the bridge.* (1936). Painted wood and stuffed cloth, 5¾″ high x 19″ long x 8¾″ wide. Collection Mr. and Mrs. Morton G. Neumann, Chicago

Ernst: *Loplop Introduces.* 1932. Pasted paper, watercolor, pencil, photograph, 19⅝x25⅜″. Collection Mr. and Mrs. E. A. Bergman, Chicago

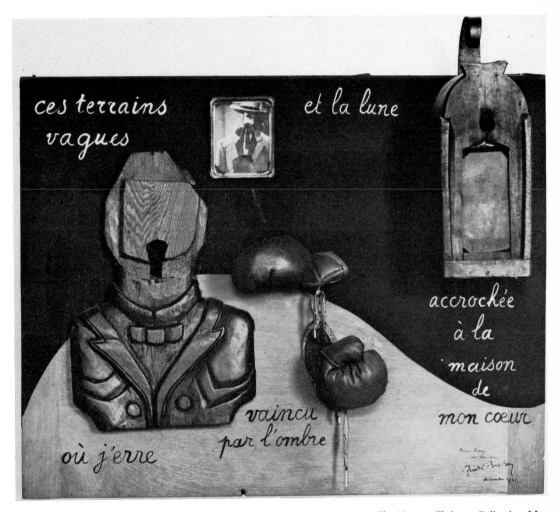

Breton: *Objet-poème*. 1941. Wood and miscellaneous objects, 18¼″ high x 21⅛″ wide x 4⅜″ deep. Collection Mrs. Yves Tanguy, Woodbury, Connecticut

Cornell: *Space Object Box.* (1959). Wooden construction with painted wood, metal rods and ring, cork ball, cordial glass containing marble, starfish, pasted paper, 9½″ high x 15″ wide x 3¾″ deep. Ferus Gallery, Los Angeles

Joseph Cornell's serene and exquisite boxes are journeys into an enchanted universe that also has the reality of this world. The evocative and mysterious poetry arising from this severely balanced work is that of the marvelous, of paradox and enigma, of questions without answers and answers without questions. The boxes are not collections of fetishes, but treasuries. They contain the hermetic secrets of a silent and discreet Magus, disguised as a game full of delightful humor and playful irony. They are autonomous allegories providing a discovery of the past, present and future; an endless complex of ideas and associations.

It is no coincidence that Cornell has selected astrological charts and astronomical maps for many of his boxes, for the sun, the moon, and the planets which govern objects and men also reveal the knowl-edge of the universe. Sole master of this domain, he defies all law or tradition. His hieratic talismans are like the highly treasured possessions of a child — anything: a Haitian postage stamp, a clay pipe, a compass, even the Night.

Despite an aura of renunciation and isolation, the magic of these boxes is not Faustian or "black," but natural and filled with love. Cornell's work stands as a crystalline refuge from a world of frustrated hopes and increasing complexity, from an impersonal world that has forgotten the magic and mystery of poetry. Lost illusions are sheltered along with pristine innocence and the pure naïveté of childhood. Within these boxes is preserved the world of soap bubbles, Hans Christian Andersen, carrousels, Queen Mab, and Ondine. They protect the penny arcades, nickelodeons, daguerrotypes, mont-

Cornell: *Medici Slot Machine*. 1942. Compartmented wooden box, with pasted illustrations and various objects, 15½″ high x 12″ wide x 4⅜″ deep. Collection Mr. and Mrs. Bernard J. Reis, New York

Cornell: *Blériot*. (1956). Box containing painted wooden trapeze supported by rusted steel spring, 18½″ high x 11¼″ wide x 4¾″ deep. Collection Mrs. Eleanor Ward, New York

Cornell: *Habitat Group for a Shooting Gallery*. 1943. Cabinet containing colored cutouts of parrots, printed cards and papers, etc., behind shattered glass, 15½″ high x 11⅛″ wide x 4¼″ deep. Ferus Gallery, Los Angeles

golfiers, stereoscopes, dioramas, and the ideal world of beauty in the silent film. How safe seem the Medici princes and princesses, Orion, Toussaint L'Ouverture, the "Grand Hôtel Fontaine de Réputation Universelle," and Taglioni dancing for an audience of one, on a panther's skin spread over the snow beneath the stars.

Joseph Cornell is also guardian of dovecotes and aviaries, of immaculate cockatoos, of exotically plumed parrots and humming-birds, and of brilliant butterflies.

His poetry of recollection and desire transcends eccentric nostalgia or excessive romanticism. Realizing what is present we are also aware of the infinity of what is absent. The emptiness of some boxes,

some with uncoiled clock springs, perches which some rare bird has deserted, glass neatly fractured by a bullet, or the sands of the sea and of Time, becomes a grave and desperate warning. Cornell's assertion of purity and of paradox is basic and human. His art is as enduring as it is ephemeral, as sophisticated and imaginative as it is innocent and simple, as universal and real as it is mysterious and personal, as wise and serious as it is witty and ironic.

It is easy to fall under the spell of such a magician and seer.

K. L. McShine
New York, 1961

Cornell: *Night Skies: Auriga.* (ca. 1954). Box containing painted wooden construction with pasted paper, 19¼″ high x 13½″ wide x 7½″ deep. Collection Mr. and Mrs. E. A. Bergman, Chicago

Cornell: *Apothecary.* 1950. Wooden cabinet with glass jars containing various objects, and liquid and dry materials, in glass compartments, 15⅞″ high x 11⅞″ wide x 4⅝″ deep. Collection Mr. and Mrs. Jean de Menil, Houston, Texas

Photograph by Herbert Loebel

THE COLLAGE ENVIRONMENT

For Simon Rodia, an immigrant tilesetter living in Watts, a slum section of Los Angeles, to have constructed his wondrously colorful towers of concrete and scrap (page 77), a knowledge of cubist *papiers collés*, the collages of Schwitters, or surrealist objects was, to say the least, unnecessary. No mode of creation is more direct or naturally arrived at than the accumulation and agglomeration of materials found close at hand. Indeed, some of the finest assemblages are the work of primitives and folk artists. Without evidence, therefore, one should not assume an artist to be familiar with his apparent precursors. On the other hand, one does not expect people as sophisticated as Duchamp, Miró, Cornell, Nevelson, or Rauschenberg to be innocent of history; there is truth in Robert Motherwell's statement that "every intelligent painter carries the whole culture of modern painting in his head."[70] But art does not always derive from art. Artists draw sustenance from everywhere: from the totality — moral, intellectual, and temporal as well as physical and sensory — of their environment and experience. In the desire to "do something big," which led Simon Rodia to thumb through the Encyclopaedia Britannica seeking out biographies of conquerors and heroes, he is surely a man of his time; and in his decision to realize this ambition by transforming the copious waste of an industrial society into structures of soaring magnificence, he found a means as contemporaneous as his compulsion. Perhaps Rodia remembered Italian mosaics but, as far as one can tell, for him environment and need supplanted tradition.

Speaking generally, we know that if the events discussed in the earlier chapters of this book had not occurred, many recent works of assemblage would not exist. But an interpretation based on temporal sequence can be false: the collages and objects of Picasso, Man Ray, Duchamp, Schwitters, Miró, and Cornell exist in the present, not the past; like newspapers, buildings, fields, beaches, or current events they are part of an artist's environment, and it is because of a special affinity between many levels and aspects of the present that the earlier works of assemblage have unexpectedly acquired a new luster.

Although the history of collage is primarily urban, in assembled art natural materials are as common as "junk" or newer manufactured objects. Did not most of us feel our first naïve delight in "found objects" on the beach or in the forest? One cannot separate even "untouched" nature from the medium of assemblage. Constructions of shells, seeds, the wings and bodies of birds and insects, human skulls, and other striking natural objects make up the bulk of primitive assemblage; displayed between pages of books, framed, arranged in cases, or placed under glass bells for scientific, educational, and aesthetic reasons, assemblages of every known species of flora, fauna, and mineral are so common as not to be noticed; the display of driftwood, its fabrication into lamps, and its incorporation into flower arrangements have become hackneyed; stridently tasteless agglomerations of sea shells, coral, and similar materials are a commonplace of tourist bazaars. Many works illustrated in the following pages employ natural components; and the interest, not only of assemblers, but of painters as well, in materials that are (or appear to be) weathered, torn, faded, broken, and otherwise enriched by deterioration and fragmentation calls attention to the interaction of man and nature as one of the richest underlying themes of modern art. Nevertheless, from cubism and futurism, Duchamp and Schwitters, to the present, the tradition of assemblage has been predominantly urban in emphasis.

The English critic Lawrence Alloway, one of the most eloquent spokesmen for composite art, has applied to it the term "junk culture":

> Junk culture is city art. Its source is obsolescence, the throwaway material of cities, as it collects in drawers, cupboards, attics, dustbins, gutters, waste lots, and city dumps. Objects have a history: first they are brand new goods; then they are possessions, accessible to few, subjected, often, to intimate and repeated use; then, as waste, they are scarred by use but available again. . . . Assemblages of such material come at the spectator as bits of life, bits of the environment. The urban environment is present, then, as the source of objects, whether transfigured or left alone.[71]

Although Alloway's criticism sometimes has a partisan ring, one must agree that the proper backdrop for recent assemblage is the multifarious fabric of the modern city — its random patchwork of slickness and deterioration, cold planning and liberating confusion, resplendent beauty and noxious squalor. The cityscape gives striking evidence of the world-wide collision of moralities and panaceas, facts and propagandas, and sets in relief the countless images — tender, comic, tragic, or drably neutral

— of contemporary life. In the past, the great determinants of the arts were nature, man, and God. For the twentieth century a fourth must be added: the artifact.

Early in the century, Apollinaire had urged poets to model their freedom on the daily newspaper "which, on a single sheet, treats the most diverse matters and ranges over distant countries,"[72] and de Chirico saw the city as an outdoor still life. Though the various decades have seen it quite differently, the collage landscape resembles that against which Italian futurism appeared: ". . . those aspects of Milan that could have been duplicated in contemporary New York, London, Berlin, Moscow, Barcelona — even Vienna or Paris,"[73] but enlarged and multiplied in the terms of a post-atomic age. On a scale of complexity so much more expanded than that of Apollinaire and Marinetti as to make comparison unnecessary, we live in a world in which a million differing realities collide, far too many for us to digest. Sheer quantity, diversity, and contradiction make a carefully partitioned impression impossible. One is forced to choose between parochialism, sweeping renunciations, or an apprehension of reality in fragments from which truth, or some semblance of it, may arise.

The city — New York above all others — has become a symbol of modern existence. The tempo of Manhattan, both as subject and conditioning milieu, has been instrumental in forming the art of our time. John Marin wrote about and painted a New York that, like a work of art, was "a thing alive." In a foreword of five packed paragraphs written in 1912 for an exhibition catalogue, he summarized the effect that New York was to exert on both American and European artists.[74] Mondrian's arrival in New York was instrumental in his change from an elemental abstraction to a style that, at the time of his death, was expanding toward complication, inclusiveness, and urban dynamism.

The connection of New York with world art during and after the second World War has become history. New York's vernacular power, its garish affront to tranquillity and taste, was a major component of abstract expressionism. Willem de Kooning's paintings of female figures were an incarnation of the city. In developing these canvases, he worked with drawings which were "cut apart, reversed, exchanged and otherwise manipulated on the painting."[75] When he placed a lipsticked mouth clipped from a color advertisement in the center of a sheet that was to become an oil study, de Kooning set the tone of the new collage. His heroine of the 1950s was the commercialized darling of the movies, the bar stool, and the sex magazine, the indulgent strumpet that fills the daydreams of a million wishful males. Juxtaposition — taking form in neocubist fractures and misalignments which often resulted from the use of actual collage techniques — has played a considerable part in de Kooning's development. In his totally committed battle between pure art and the street, in his examination of hypnotizing details in tabloid photographs, and in the transfer of newsprint to pigment (in such pictures as *Gotham News*), de Kooning recorded the impact of commercial culture on postwar art. Although he was surely not an isolated voice, he intensified the interest in "pop culture" — in the expendable art and literature that became so important as a subject for Rauschenberg, Johns, Conner, and so many subsequent, but usually less skillful, painters and assemblers. For a new generation and in another spirit, de Kooning's adulterative gesture may have had an effect not unlike Picasso's in 1912.

de Kooning: *Study for Woman.* (1950). Oil on paper with pasted mouth, 14⅝x11⅝".
Private collection, New York

To believers in the superiority of small community life, carefully balanced in the interest of an ideal existence for hypothetical family units, the uncontrolled growth of large cities has appeared, not without reason, as a frightening encroachment on nature and natural man. Planners like Mumford and Wright have decried the squalor of urban concentration and the wasteland that has all but swallowed not only untouched nature, but the rural community as well. This "rurban" environment is truly a collage landscape: an unplanned assemblage of animated gasoline displays, screaming billboards, hundred-mile-an-hour automobiles jammed bumper to bumper, graveyards of twisted and rusting scrap, lots strewn with bed springs and cracked toilet bowls. Quite justly the intellectuals and socially conscious photographers and painters of the 1930s saw the urban complex as a blight and as an offense against human dignity. Industrialism, capitalist callousness, and lack of planning were properly cited as the causes of squalor and degradation.

Yet, more than forty years after Duchamp's first "readymades" and Schwitters' discovery of the loveliness of refuse, by an unconscious acceptance of the dada proposition of reversibility, the caustic portrayal of the city presented by Henry Miller's *Air-Conditioned Nightmare* of 1945, has become, for a new generation of artists, a fulfillment of the glittering MERZ environment of Schwitters' imagination. Such an inversion, from ugliness to beauty, can transpose sociological and utilitarian reformism into complete aesthetic acceptance. The world of artifacts can be seen (as Monet sought to see nature) with a vision freed from conceptual preconditioning. The peeling *décollage* on abandoned billboards in the blighted neighborhoods of Chicago or Jersey City, accented by the singing colors and clean edges of emblems intended to sell cigarettes and beer, or the rubble of fallen New York tenements piled between walls patterned in flowered pinks and blues, can take on an intense beauty more poignant than that of the lacerated posters and graffiti that cover the old walls of Rome and Paris. By contrast, the hygienic uniformity of garden suburbs and the glass-curtained propriety of Park Avenue or Lake Shore Drive seem drab and monotonous: the deadening imprint of arbitrary planning on the interplay of life. It is of interest, at the very least, to see a recent *Mildew Manifesto Against Rationalism in Architecture* issued amid the prosperity of postwar Germany, calling for the salvation of "functional architecture from moral ruin" by pouring "a disintegrating medium over the clean glass and concrete walls, so that the mildew can establish itself there. . . ."[76]

Rodia: *The Watts Towers* (highest tower about 100 feet high). Los Angeles, ca. 1921-1954

I have nobody to help me out. I was a poor man. Had to do a little at a time. Nobody helped me. I think if I hire a man he don't know what to do. A million times I don't know what to do myself. I never had a single helper. Some of the people say what was he doing . . . some of the people think I was crazy and some people said I was going to do something.

I wanted to do something in the United States because I was raised here you understand? I wanted to do something for the United States because there are nice people in this country.

— SIMON RODIA

The Watts Towers, *Los Angeles,*
The Committee for Simon Rodia's Towers in Watts

The Watts Towers were built by an Italian tilesetter, Simon Rodia, of steel rods, wire screening and concrete, broken dishes and colored glass, pieces of green Seven-Up, blue milk of magnesia, and other bottles, fragments of mirror, shells, and a variety of stones and other mineral substances. Singlehanded, and without preparatory drawings, scaffolding, or machine equipment, he labored on the Towers for thirty-three years. From the flat surroundings of dusty streets, one-story habitations, vacant lots, and railroad tracks that make up the drab neighborhood of Watts in Los Angeles, the three spires ascend in a concentric tracery as logical and weightless in appearance as the last Gothic architecture. On approaching their odd site, pointed like the prow of a ship, one's eyes slowly discover with delight that the maze of structural members, the surrounding wall, and within it

the labyrinth of loggias, fountains, benches, and other imaginative motifs that make up the complex, glow and vibrate in an extraordinary mosaic of color, line, and pattern.

To dismiss this unique creation as a quaint folly — as one more bizarre production of an eccentric folk artist — would be an error. Less capricious than many of Gaudí's structures, Rodia's Towers are much more than uncontrolled accretions of junk. His innate artistry is evident everywhere in masterful contrasts and analogies of sizes and textures, man-made and natural materials, organic and geometric form, monochromatic and complementary color schemes, and opacity and transparency. From the brilliant collages of broken dishes, cup handles project outward, inviting the touch, and patterned fragments are sharply set against soft flat tones; as in Byzantine mosaics or the pointillist paintings of Seurat, touches of red or orange enliven large fields of varied blues or greens. Rodia separated soft-drink bottles melted in the incinerator from those cleanly broken, to make homogeneous compositions of swirling forms. Against assembled panels, lunettes, and finials, he placed other units varying in size and color, or uncovered areas of concrete in which the design is built up by impressions from tools, cookie molds, corncobs, and even projecting casts from boots and shoes. On a larger scale of relationship, these elements and groups are harmonized with the total structure. The patterned pavements, as beautiful in their rhythmic line, pale colors, and varied repetition as those of Spain or South America, have

Rodia: Details of The Watts Towers

designs resulting from multiplied impressions of scrap ironwork.

In 1954, stopping just short of realizing his dream, Rodia left Los Angeles permanently for a secluded life in northern California. Except for a tiny circle whose admiration finally took form in The Committee for Simon Rodia's Towers in Watts, his life work has been ignored, condemned, or ridiculed. If it were not for the Committee's persistent and dedicated battle against municipal callousness, in fact, the Towers would have been intentionally and completely destroyed in the name of civic improvement. Yet even in the damaged condition which has resulted from neglect and juvenile destructiveness, the Watts Towers are a unique creation of inspiring power and beauty, a masterpiece of assemblage.

Rodia: Detail of The Watts Towers

The memory throws up high and dry
A crowd of twisted things;
A twisted branch upon the beach
Eaten smooth, and polished
As if the world gave up
The secret of its skeleton,
Stiff and white.
A broken spring in a factory yard,
Rust that clings to the form that the strength has left
Hard and curled and ready to snap.

T. S. ELIOT [77]

The catalogue of the exhibition (page 153) lists the materials incorporated in each work. It suggests the limitless diversity that relates assembled art to the world. The finished works, moreover, are usually closer to everyday life than either abstract or representational art. Such objects as Victor Brauner's *Wolf-Table* (page 64), Edward Kienholz' *Jane Doe* (page 134), or George Herms' *The Poet* (page 133), however arresting, strange, or poetic may be their effect, resemble furniture more than they do sculpture; they fit more naturally in a living room than they do in a museum. A similar shortening of psychological distance results from the treatment of materials: one's hand is drawn toward the frayed holes in Burri's sacks (pages 136-137) as unconsciously as toward a tear in a pair of trousers.

Intrinsic to the medium of assemblage is an entirely new relationship between work and spectator: a reconquest, but by different means, of the realism that abstract art replaced. In 1915 (for an exhibition at the Tanner Gallery in Zurich) Jean Arp spoke out "against illusion, fame, artifice, copy or plagiarism," and "for reality, the precision of the indefinable, rigorous precision." The participating artists, he said later, "were disgusted with oil painting and were searching for new materials." [78] It was perhaps Picasso's unwillingness to take this step to complete abstractness that led him, in 1923, to assert that an artist must know how to "convince others of the truthfulness of his lies." [79]

Even Gris, who composed "flat architecture" in entirely nonrepresentational forms, chose to overlay his abstraction with realism: to "adjust the white so that it becomes a paper and the black so that it becomes a shadow." [80] When he interpolated illustrations, pieces of mirror, or typographical clippings, replacing a deductive image by a fragment of the environment, the metaphysic of juxtaposition was barely posed: the reality problem raised by assemblage is a new and different one that has little to do with illusionism or *trompe-l'oeil* devices. When the scene behind the gold frame came forward and began to crack up or fade out (as it did in Mondrian's art of 1910-1915), abstract pictorial elements became more "real" than what they represented, and the gap between painting and sculpture narrowed until, in the abstract *tableaux-objets* that followed, the distinction was almost obliterated. Abstract

de la Villeglé: *6 Bd. Poissonnière*. 1957. Torn
paper posters, 34⅝x23¼". Galerie J, Paris

painting and sculpture substituted a second reality, self-contained and objective,
for the surrogate reality of illusionism. Not only did it narrow the gap between flat
and three-dimensional media, but also that between art and everyday life. A final
step, from art to the presentation of objects assembled in ordinary daily acts and
without aesthetic intention, is taken in Daniel Spoerri's "snare pictures" (pages 9,
132). Often dramatic and perceptually compelling, they are "situations prepared by
chance,"[81] selected, glued together, and presented vertically rather than horizontally.
"Spoerri doesn't pretend to create works of art," Alain Jouffroy writes, "nor does
he proclaim that his works exalt non-art or anti-art."[82] In precisely the same spirit,
Mimmo Rotella, Raymond Hains, and the other salvagers of lacerated posters
(pages 108-109) rip down portions of the environment and present them as pictures.
The critic Pierre Restany has dubbed this group "the new realists." "What they offer
us," he writes, "is an entire aspect of the real, captured in its objective integrity,
without transcription of any sort. Never, at any moment is it a question of re-crea-
tion, but on the contrary of an expressive transmutation."[83] However one chooses to
categorize them, the assemblages exhibited by these men should be compared to

those in which the arrangement is the result of "art" rather than accident and choice. The challenge that Duchamp presented to our minds when he exhibited a bottle rack and a urinal — a challenge compounded in Spoerri's project for a combined grocery store and art gallery where each avocado pear, yam, and bottle of olives would be labeled ATTENTION: WORK OF ART — should not be side-stepped.

Just such extreme actualism — i.e., the inclusion of a Coca-Cola bottle rather than the representation of one — is intrinsic to assemblage; but it points to only one layer of meaning, and only certain works exemplify it sharply or purely. In thought-provoking ways assemblage is poetic rather than realistic, for each constituent element can be transformed. Physical materials and their auras are transmuted into a new amalgam that both transcends and includes its parts. When, as in a primitive cult object, a shell becomes a human eye because of its context, the accepted hierarchy of categories (as the surrealists delighted in pointing out) is disrupted. When the meanings of highly charged units impinge on a poetic as well as on a physical or visual level, significant expression becomes possible.

The assembler, therefore, can be both a metaphysician and (because his units are loosely related rather than expository) a poet who mingles attraction and repulsion, natural and human identification, ironic or naïve responses. Because overtones and associations as well as physical materials are placed in juxtaposition, it could almost be said that a constellation of meanings can exist independently of the colors, textures, and forms which are its carriers. In fact, three levels of operation can be specified: that of tangible materials, that of vision, at which colors and other formal qualities alter each other and blend like tastes or scents, and finally that of "literary" meanings. " . . . many diverse images, borrowed from very different orders of things," Bergson wrote in his *Introduction to Metaphysics*, "may, by the convergence of their action, direct the consciousness to the precise point where there is a certain intuition

Anonymous: *Two-Headed Dog*. Cabinda, Africa. 19th century. Carved wood, nails, animal teeth, 11x22¾". Musée de l'homme, Paris

to be seized. By choosing images as dissimilar as possible, we shall prevent any one of them from usurping the place of the intuition it is intended to call up. . . ."[84]

Certain works of assemblage, with an attraction like that of green-encrusted bronzes or the unnamable artifacts of a people far away or long dead, seem to emit a magical halo: an aura too ephemeral to be ascribed to sensory stimuli, but so existent as to seem measurable. Unfortunately it is on this level (that of wizardry as well as art) that the value of a work can easily be missed or misinterpreted. It is one of the limitations of civilized human beings to be more readily convinced by syllogistic discourse than by words or forms poetically related: it is easy to disbelieve what is written in a plastic language.

Figuratively, the practice of assemblage raises materials from the level of formal relations to that of associational poetry, just as numbers and words, on the contrary, tend to be formalized. Transmutation tends also to move in the opposite direction in abstract-expressionist painting, in which the subject is absorbed into the medium. But when textures and tones totally created by the artist take on a tactile or visual effect of actuality — as do the graffiti, "texturologies," and "topographies" of Dubuffet, the "rhinoceros hide" surfaces of Jan Lebenstein, the carved wood surfaces of Lucio Muñoz, or the relief paintings of Tàpies — the two tendencies, which might be called "radiative" and "absorptive," meet. In the assemblages of Wagemaker, Bouras, Tumarkin, and others, assertive plastic substances provide a field into which *objets trouvés* are pressed.

Assemblage is a method with disconcertingly centrifugal potentialities. It is metaphysical and poetic as well as physical and realistic. When paper is soiled or lacerated, when cloth is worn, stained, or torn, when wood is split, weathered, or patterned with peeling coats of paint, when metal is bent or rusted, they gain connotations which unmarked materials lack. More specific associations are denoted when an object can be identified as the sleeve of a shirt, a dinner fork, the leg of a rococo chair, a doll's eye or hand, an automobile bumper, or a social security card. In both situa-

Arman: *Arteriosclerosis.* 1961. Forks and spoons in glass-covered box, 18¾" high x 28⅝" wide x 3" deep. Galleria Schwarz, Milan

tions meaning and material merge. Identities drawn from diverse contexts and levels of value are confronted not only physically, within the limits of the work they form, but metaphysically and associationally, within (and modified by) the unique sensibility of the spectator. Even taken in isolation, the possible meanings of objects and fragments are infinitely rich, whereas (except in special cases like that of John Flannagan, whose images conform to the natural contours of stones and boulders) professional art materials such as paint, plastic, stone, bronze, etc., are formless and, in the Platonic sense, are pure essences of redness, hardness, or ductility. Found materials are works already in progress: prepared for the artist by the outside world, previously formed, textured, colored, and even sometimes entirely prefabricated into accidental "works of art."

John Chamberlain's decision to work with sections of scrap automobile bodies and other painted metal (see page 138) solved the problem of polychromy in sculpture at one stroke. The use of non-art materials has put an unprecedented range of new formal qualities at the artist's disposal; but unless he carefully obliterates marks of the origin and history of each element, these qualities inevitably transcend abstractness of form, texture, and color. It goes without saying that modes of fabrication and varieties of craftsmanship also relate to content. Tearing, cutting, burning, pasting, stapling, nailing, sewing, welding, and the use of heavy plastic substances can do much more than separate or join. Expressive neatness or sloppiness of craftsmanship ranges from the oversolidity of H. C. Westermann's *About a Black Magic Maker* to the loose works of experimenters like Kaprow or Whitman whose fluttering creations of newspaper and rags, doctrinaire in their fragility, are barely joined to each other at all. The raw construction of Jean Tinguely's demented machines provides a large part of their expressive power, and Edward Kienholz (a cabinetmaker by trade) ironically hides the thoroughness of his craftsmanship behind an appearance of sloppy workmanship. At the other pole of this spectrum one is moved by the feminine delicacy with which the fragile and transparent materials of Anne Ryan are overlaid, and the ephemeral precision of Joseph Cornell's boxes.

The function of materials in assemblage cannot be explained in terms appropriate for orthodox media. In *papiers collés* such as *Bottle of Suze* (frontispiece), Picasso used printed matter simply to get a gray tone, as so many other collagists have done since; where the type is larger, it provides an oscillating pattern. But Apollinaire sanctioned the use of numbers and letters as pictorial elements because, although "new in art, they are already soaked in humanity."[85] Whether it can be read or not, a fragment of newsprint has a wholly different meaning from the page of an old book, a crumbling and yellowed manuscript, a political poster, or a legal document. Its message may be central to the work's theme, as is the news clipping included in Boccioni's *Cavalry Charge* (page 30), or, as in Schwitters' word-fragment MERZ, it can carry the challenge of a manifesto.

The expansion of this idea beyond typography to include the entire range of materials and objects postulates endless possibilities. If they are to be even partially assessed, it is necessary to consider the multiplicity of meanings and implications that lie between garish newness and total disintegration, artifact and natural form, machine and hand fabrication, or between socially esteemed and tabooed objects.

The fabric of meaning woven by materials can cover the distant in time and

Westermann: *About a Black Magic Maker*. (1959-60). Slot machine of imitation wood grain containing miscellaneous objects, 72″ high x 42″ wide. Allan Frumkin Gallery, New York

space, awakening a romantic response to ruins, architectural and sculptural fragments, and the evocative richness of old walls or ritual vessels. As element is set beside element, the many qualities and auras of isolated fragments are compounded, fused, or contradicted so that — by their own confronted volitions as it were — physical matter becomes poetry. Directed, intentionally or unconsciously, by an artist's intellectual position, emotional predisposition, or any other conditioning attitude or coloration, a vast repertoire of expression — exultant, bitter, ironic, erotic, or lyrical — can be achieved by means different in kind from that of painting and sculpture, but akin to those of literature.

An artist, as Marcel Duchamp has emphasized,[86] is never more than partially cognizant of what his work communicates. Whatever his intention may be, he cannot side-step the symbolic meaning of objects, nor can his audience. Collagists from Gris to Man Ray, Cornell, Cohen, and Baj have employed mirrors. Who can ignore the fascination of this strange object that dissolves its own surface but brings into being a counterpart of the real world? How can its presence in a work of art not carry something of the potency that it had for the primitive mind? Of the myth of Narcissus? Of the childhood delight in Alice's liberation from everyday life? Of the incantation that begins: "Mirror, mirror, on the wall"? Of one's discovery of infinity in "barber-shop" reflections? Of the daily mystery of confronting one's self in reverse?

The history of assemblage, from Picasso and Man Ray on, is punctured with the sharp points of nails. Used expressively, how can they fail to elicit at least a tremor of the meaning they have in a thousand crucifixions painted between the sixth and twentieth centuries? Forks, knives, dishes, and other eating utensils, playing cards, ropes, flags, clocks, shoes, wheels — these objects contain immeasurable layers of significance. Dolls and mannequins, common in surrealist objects, used by George Cohen during the fifties, and recently by Kienholz, Conner, and many others, elicit a range of references which can be erotic, ludicrous, or horrible; separate parts of the body, as in Cohen's *Anybody's Self-Portrait* (page 112) or Arman's *Little Hands* (page 127), can stir unrealized emotions frightening to contemplate. John Latham works almost exclusively with old books: revered or feared, for centuries treasured or burned, how can one imagine their full potential as expressive form and symbol? These examples are few, but they serve as a passing allusion to the enormous variety of subject matter accessible to an assembler: an unending reverberation of object-meanings that, because of their associations, reach back to the origins of human consciousness and to the depth of human personality.

Man Ray: *Mr. Knife and Miss Fork.* 1944. Knife and fork, wooden beads, net-covered embroidery frame, on cloth, 13⅜x9⅜". Galerie Rive Droite, Paris

ATTITUDES AND ISSUES

Assemblage is a new medium. It is to be expected, therefore, that it should be the carrier of developing viewpoints for which orthodox techniques are less appropriate. It has indeed provided an effective outlet for artists of a generation weaned on abstract expressionism but unwilling to mannerize Pollock, de Kooning, or other masters whom they admire. Because of their concern for subject matter, painting and sculpture are not their only influences. Many cultivate attitudes that could be labeled "angry," "beat," or "sick"; they inherit a malaise shared by authors such as Kafka, Sartre, Beckett, and Ionesco. Certain of their attitudes are comparable to those of the dada period; but why (especially considering the overtone of tired academicism which it can imply) is the prefix "neo" more applicable in 1961 than it was in 1921? Social and emotional life is scarcely more secure at present than it was during the youth of Jarry, Vaché, Schwitters, or Duchamp.

The current wave of assemblage owes at least as much to abstract expressionism (with its dada and surrealist components) as it does to dada directly, but it is nevertheless quite differently oriented: it marks a change from a subjective, fluidly abstract art toward a revised association with environment. The method of juxtaposition is an appropriate vehicle for feelings of disenchantment with the slick international idiom that loosely articulated abstraction has tended to become, and the social values that this situation reflects. The technique of collage has always been a threat to the approved media of oil painting, carving, and casting. Inherent in Kurt Schwitters' MERZ collages, objects, environments, and activities (which, in various ways, all incorporated the spectator and the life around him into the fabric and structure of the work) was an impatience with the line that separated art from life. The medium of which Schwitters must be recognized as *le grand maître*, still expanding after more than forty years, cannot be dismissed as the affectation of a group of incompetents. It is an established mode of communication employing words, symbols, and signs, as freely as it does pigments, materials, and objects. Wordlessly associative, it has added to abstract art the vernacular realism that both Ingres and Mondrian sought to exclude by the process of abstraction.

Assemblage has become, temporarily at least, the language for impatient, hypercritical, and anarchistic young artists. With it, or admixtures of it with painting and sculpture, they have given form to content drawn from popular culture: more recent equivalents, as the English critic Reyner Banham argues, of Boccioni's love of "all anti-art manifestations of our epoch — café-chantant, gramaphone, cinema, electric advertising, mechanistic architecture, skyscrapers . . . nightlife . . . speed, automobiles, aeroplanes and so forth."[87]

For the first time since the period of the futurists, the automobile, for example, has been effectively dealt with by the plastic arts, but with an emotional tone that is not at all the same. By now, the automobile has become a mass killer, the upholstered love-boat of the adolescent, and the status symbol of the socially disenfranchised. In our period the impact of these "insolent chariots" is at least as great as previously was that of the horse — whose role as a living symbol could be said to have ended with the agonized scream of the disemboweled victim in Picasso's *Guernica*. In the magnificent bronze of 1951, *Baboon and Young*, Picasso used a miniature automobile body to simulate the head of an ape.

It is no longer delight with mechanization that is represented. John Chamberlain salvages smashed, bent, and rusted car bodies, but only, he says, for their color and form. Jason Seley uses nothing but bumpers, and as a counterforce to the elegance of his compositions, he emphasizes their previous function. César takes a *méchant* pleasure in seeing devicerated auto-body shells compressed into dense blocks of steel collage. James Dine, in a "happening" named *Car Crash*, and in a series of gouaches and collages, has dealt with the automobile as a symbol of love and death. Richard Hamilton, an English artist who admires Marcel Duchamp, juxtaposes the forms of female models with those of Chryslers and electric kitchen equipment. William Copley, an American surrealist painter working in France, draws attention to the comic gaudiness and erotic symbolism of the automobile. Larry Rivers paints the front ends of Buicks. In addition to plumbing and other scrap metal, Richard Stankiewicz uses cylinder blocks and tire chains to make satiric personages or carefully structured abstract assemblages.

The themes beginning to pass through the doors of art museums are (once again, as in the days of Courbet) those described by Gide as "the squalor of reality."[88] Or, in a more current — and perhaps therefore a more apt — phrase, Allan Kaprow speaks of "the nameless sludge and whirl of urban events."[89] All is not grumbling, "jazz," and "kicks," however: it is not hard to discern behind these vernacular

Mesens: *Mouvement immobile*. 1960. Cut and pasted papers with ink, on cardboard, 13x21½″. Grosvenor Gallery, London

subjects a striving, embittered by disenchantment, but mystical and moral as well as irascible and sexual. It is in part an outcome of insecurity that is more than economic, and of the aesthetic individualism that, following the failure of liberal politics during the thirties and forties, provided a motive force for abstract expressionism.

The vernacular repertoire includes beat Zen and hot rods, mescalin experiences and faded flowers, photographic bumps and grinds, the *poubelle* (i.e., trash can), juke boxes, and hydrogen explosions. Such subjects are often approached in a mystical, aesthetic, or "arty" way, but just as often they are fearfully dark, evoking horror or nausea: the anguish of the scrap heap; the images of charred bodies that keep Hiroshima and Nagasaki before our eyes; the confrontation of democratic platitudes with the Negro's disenfranchisement; the travesty of the Chessman trial. Indeed, in the United States, a network of artists could be identified who, quite independently and with no political affiliation, incorporate or represent in their work flags, shields, eagles, and other symbols of democracy, national power, and authority, with mild amusement or irony, with unconcealed resentment and scatalogical bitterness, or simply as totally banal images.

Adjunctive to the identification with popular culture, but more whimsical, is a group of objects whose elements can be manipulated, removed, added to, or reassembled by the spectator: these elements include balls that drop, playing cards that can be moved from hook to hook, boxes and openings from which mementos can be removed and replaced by others, tablets on which notes may be written, or toy pianos that can be played. The spectator is invited to be a participant in a childlike sort of game.

Another group of works, related to the international trend toward mobile constructions in the tradition of Duchamp, Moholy-Nagy, Gabo, and Calder, combines assemblage with mechanical movement.

"Resist the anxious fear to fix the instantaneous, to kill that which is living," warns Jean Tinguely, whose most recent work, influenced by Rauschenberg and Stankiewicz, fuses the tradition of kinetic art with that of assemblage.[90] On a dank evening in March 1960, Tinguely's "self-constructing and self-destroying work of art," *Homage to New York* (white and stately five minutes before its maiden performance, and compounded of a mélange of materials ranging from bicycle wheels and dishpans to an upright piano), vibrated and gyrated, painted pictures, played music, and magnificently but inefficiently sawed, shook, and burned itself to rubble and extinction in the sculpture garden of the Museum of Modern Art. A year or so earlier the British junk man and eccentric Gustave Metzger was making "expendable art" with acid brushed onto stretched nylon: "as the acid is applied, it dissolves in patches, the edges curl and a pattern is formed."[91] He has also proposed sculpture that will disintegrate more slowly, "by undergoing a continual destructive process such as the action of acid or some other errosive [sic]. This type of work could also be destroyed by the action of natural elements — rain and humid atmosphere under normal circumstances will almost certainly corrode completely a thin piece of iron or mild steel within a decade at the outside."[92]

Common to many of the controversial ideas, attitudes, and activities cited in the preceding paragraphs is a dissatisfaction, ranging from impatience to nihilism, with the limitations traditionally imposed by the idea of art, the sequestered atmosphere and

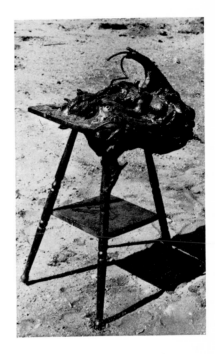

Conner: *Last Supper*. (1961). Wax, rags, etc., applied to top of wooden table, 40″ high x 20″ square. The Alan Gallery, New York

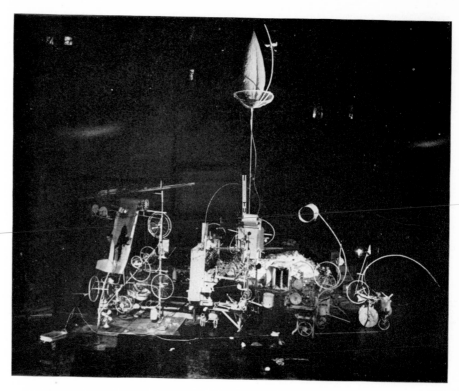

Tinguely: *Homage to New York: A self-constructing and self-destroying work of art*. Demonstration in the sculpture garden of the Museum of Modern Art, New York, March 17, 1960

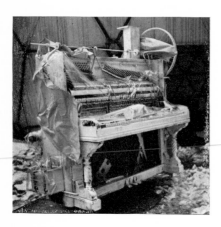

Tinguely: Piano before its incorporation into *Homage to New York*

geometric enframement of the museum, and — though the spotlight of success and fashion is constantly shifting toward allegedly avant-garde innovations — the whirl of dealers, collectors, and soaring prices. Yet, by a process of reciprocal thesis and antithesis oscillating with the speed of alternating current, a negative position needs only to be stated to be immediately countered by a return to art for its own sake within the same camp: one must surely agree with Basil Taylor that "the spirit of art — anti-art is of the greatest significance in the history of our time."[93]

Allen Kaprow, in a manuscript of 1960, "Paintings, Environments, and Happenings," advocates "a quite clear-headed decision to abandon craftsmanship and permanence," and "the use of obviously perishable media such as newspaper, string, adhesive tape, growing grass or real food," so "no one can mistake the fact that the work will pass into dust or garbage quickly."[94] The medium of refuse, according to Kaprow (but over the objections of certain of his associates), can "force once again the eternal problems of what may be (or become) art and what may not. The intellectuals' typical disdain for popular culture, for the objects and debris of mass production, is as always a clear instance of aesthetic discrimination: *this* is fit for art; *that* is not. Such high-mindedness is not at all different from the seventeenth century's

James Dine in his happening *The Car Crash*, presented at the
Reuben Gallery, New York, November, 1960

belief in the greater value of 'noble' themes over genre ones."[95]

Although the connection is far too dispersive to make precise, the productions known as "happenings," presented by Kaprow, James Dine, and other New York artists at the Reuben Gallery and elsewhere, had their origin in painting and collage. Kaprow explains their expansion from "agglomerates" to three-dimensional assemblages large enough for a spectator to enter, to become an element of, and even to alter if he chooses. Finally, surrounding and including not only their authors but their audience as well, "happenings" involve movements, costumes, sounds, lights, and scents as well as forms and colors. The producers of "happenings" have no common program, but their most evident general aim seems to be the spatialization or immobilization of time, sequence, and movement. The performances avoid climax or denouement in order to imprint a series of sharp images on the minds of the audience. Separated actions, related only by their impact on each other, take place simultaneously, leading to an effect described by a reviewer of Claes Oldenburg's *Fotodeath* as the "extended exposure of a picture."[96]

Recognizing the connection of New York "happenings" with painting, sculpture, and assemblage, and the unquestionable success of a few performances, one must nevertheless assert that, to date, many have resembled amateur theatricals. It is interesting to note, indeed, that many works of the avant-garde film and the professional theater have an analogous antinarrational tendency which could be described, in its avoidance of a definite conclusion, by the advice André Gide gives himself in his "Journal" of *The Counterfeiters:* "This novel will end sharply, not through exhaustion of the subject, which must give the impression of inexhaustibility, but on the contrary through its expansion and by a sort of blurring of its outline. It must not be neatly rounded off, but rather disperse, disintegrate. . . ."[97]

In quite the same way, the theme of assemblage is dispersed by the consideration of "happenings" and similar activities going on in New York and other centers throughout the world — especially when they take place in museum gardens, railroad stations, rifle ranges, Venetian gondolas, or autobuses. Certain of these events differ from the routine occurrences "outside" only in the special kind of attention which they demand.

The importance of assemblage to modern art is surely beyond question. It is nevertheless always hard to avoid judging, either positively or negatively, by extrinsic criteria: by what one supposes will be the outcome of the principles a work exemplifies, or simply by a prejudice for or against the tendency or group that it seems to represent. The challenge presented to the plastic arts by the new wave of assemblage should nevertheless not be evaded, but surely pseudo innovation should never be embraced because it seems to be *le dernier cri.* Yet the need of certain artists to defy and obliterate accepted categories, to fabricate aggressive objects, to present subjects tabooed by accepted standards, to undermine the striving for permanency by using soiled, valueless, and fragile materials, and even to present ordinary objects for examination unaltered — these manifestations are signs of vitality. They once more demonstrate the necessity for artists to flee the current circle of approval while seeking recognition on another level, to return again from abstraction to nature, to work with the materials of life rather than art.

Those who decry such developments as dishonest or deplorable, as evidence of commercialism, capitulation to jaded fashion, moral decay, or worse — and such views are held by many who are neither stubborn conservatives nor who reject venturesome art — should surely be heard. On the opposite side — Though who can honestly declare himself to be entirely in one camp or the other? — lies an unqualified faith in the purity of the regenerative human activity of art no matter where it may lead. Somewhere between these opposed prejudices lies the realization, supported by history, that Western art is, has always been, and should continue in a state of ferment and constant redefinition. And it must be recognized with approval and pleasure that, in addition to enriching and adulterating the themes and forms of painting and sculpture, makers of assembled art have wrought a truly magical transformation: from banality and ugliness, dispersion and waste, tawdriness and commercialism, they have created challenging, meaningful, and often beautiful objects ordered by principles inseparable from this century.

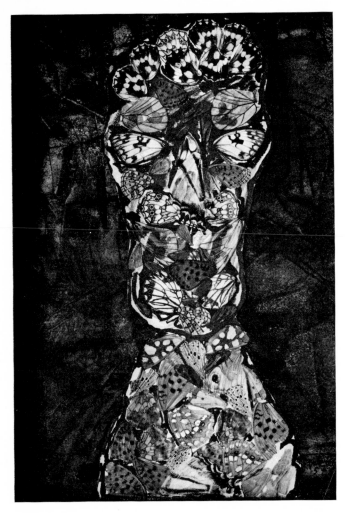

Dubuffet: *Portrait of a Man.* (1957). Butterfly wings and watercolor on cardboard, 9¾x6¼". Collection Mme Y. Silvers, Paris

In August 1953 Dubuffet made a group of small collages of butterfly wings. In November they were followed by a series of lithographs made by cutting and pasting sheets of a special paper, previously textured and spotted with lithographic ink, and transferring the resulting collages to stone for printing. The first assemblages d'empreintes were made in December by applying the same technique directly, using ordinary paper and Chinese ink. The term "assemblages" rather than "collages" was used for these works because Dubuffet felt that the term "collage" should not be applied generically to all types of pasted art, but "reserved for the collages made in the period 1910-1920 by the Dadaists, Picasso and Braque, etc." In 1954 he extended the method into three dimensions in the "little statues of precarious life . . . made for the most part of assemblages of fragments of natural elements": twisted pieces of wood, sponges, clinkers, papier-mâché, and various sorts of debris. Pictures made of "botanical elements" such as orange peelings or leaves, and of course the tableaux d'assemblages in oil, assembled from canvas prepared in the same way as the earlier "imprints," are also the outcome of the first collages of butterfly wings and of the assembled lithographs.

I have always loved — it is a sort of vice — to employ only the most common materials in my work, those that one does not dream of at first because they are too crude and close at hand and seem unsuitable for anything whatsoever. I like to proclaim that my art is an enterprise to rehabilitate discredited values. . . .

JEAN DUBUFFET
Translated from the catalogue of the Dubuffet retrospective exhibition, Musèe des Arts Décoratifs, 1961, p. 48

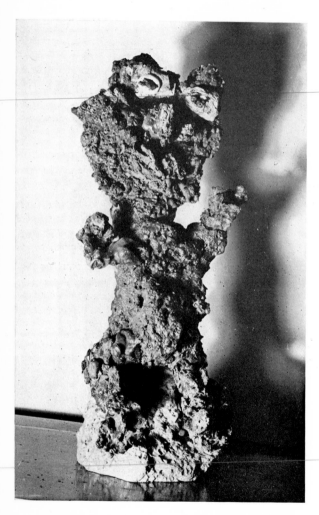

Dubuffet: *Figure.* 1954. Clinker, 16½″ high. Collection Mr. and Mrs. Harry Lewis Winston, Birmingham, Michigan

Dubuffet: *The Duke.* (1954). Sponge, 24″ high. Stephen Hahn Gallery, New York

opposite, Dubuffet: *Georges Dubuffet in the Garden.* 1956. Cut-up oil paintings on canvas, 61x36″. Collection Mr. and Mrs. William H. Weintraub, New York

Robert Motherwell has worked in collage, or combinations of collage and painting, for more than fifteen years. Among the painters who brought about the resurgence of abstract art in the United States after 1945, it is he who must be regarded as the leading exponent of the papier collé. *The following comment by Motherwell, written in 1946, bears as much on his collages of the sixties (though they are freer and more painterly) as it did on those of the forties:*

The sensation of physically operating on the world is very strong in the medium of the papier collé *or collage, in which various kinds of paper are pasted to the canvas. One cuts and chooses and shifts and pastes, and sometimes tears off and begins again. In any case, shaping and arranging such a relational structure obliterates the need, and often the awareness of representation. Without reference to likenesses, it possesses feeling because all the decisions in regard to it are ultimately made on the grounds of feeling.*[98]

Motherwell: *Pyrénéen Collage.* (1961). Oil and pasted papers, 23x30″. Owned by the artist

opposite, Motherwell: *In Grey with Parasol.* (1947). Oil, pasted papers, etc., on board, 48x36″. The New Gallery, New York

Nickle: *Collage*. (1958-59). Paper and cardboard, 20x28½". Owned by the artist

Ryan: *Number 48.* (1950). Pasted paper, etc., 15¾x12½″. The Museum of Modern Art, New York. Katharine Cornell Fund

opposite, Fine: *Sudden Encounter.* (1961). Pasted papers, watercolor, charcoal, 21¼x27¾″. Graham Gallery, New York

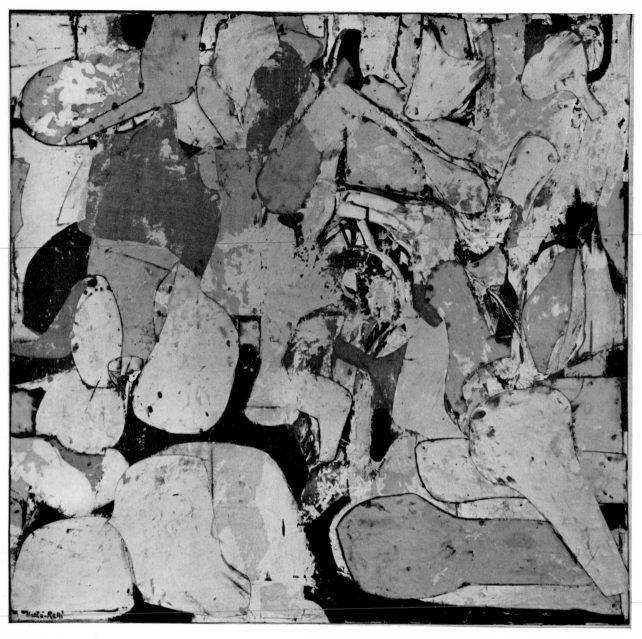

Marca-Relli: *The Snare*. (1956). Oil on cut-up canvas and cloth, 49⅛x52¾″. Collection Mr. and Mrs. Arnold H. Maremont, Chicago

Vicente: *Collage No. 10.* (1957). Pasted papers with charcoal, on board, 30x24″. André Emmerich Gallery, New York

Cooper: *Tal-lee*. 1948. Torn and pasted papers; ink, wax, 14½x22″. Gimpel Fils, London

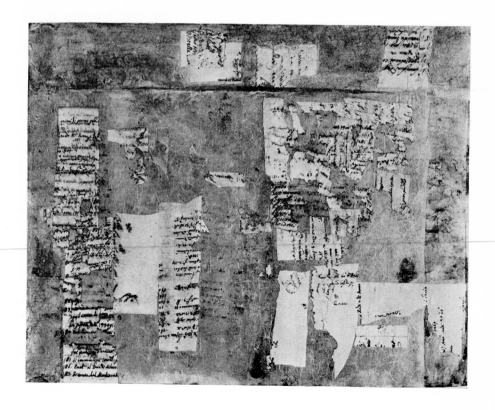

Irwin: *Collage No. IX.* (1959). Pasted papers on board, 47x34″. Collection Mr. and Mrs. Arnold H. Maremont, Chicago

opposite, Rudowicz: *Number 51.* 1960. Pasted papers on cardboard, 14x18¼″. Felix Landau Gallery, Los Angeles

Baj: *Shouting General.* (1960). Oil on canvas, with brocade, clock dials, medals, cartridge belt, water canteen, etc., 57½x45″. Galleria Schwarz, Milan

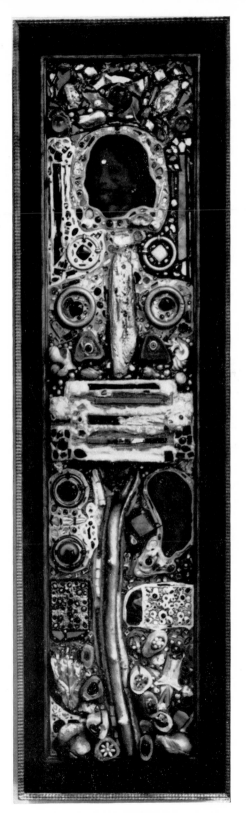

Ossorio: *Excelsior*. (1960). Illustrations and miscellaneous objects and materials, on wooden board, 56x12″. Betty Parsons Gallery, New York

Denny: *Collage*. 1957. Oil, torn paper, cloth, etc., 18x21". Owned by the artist

opposite, Getman: *Maria*. (1958). Torn paper posters on masonite, 47¼x35¼".
Collection Mr. and Mrs. Eddie Albert, Pacific Palisades, California

Rotella: *Before or After*. 1961. Torn and pasted paper posters, mounted on canvas, 59¼x32⅞". Owned by the artist

Hains: "*De Gaulle compte sur vous, aidez-le.*" (1961). Torn paper posters, 47¼x39⅜". Collection Mr. and Mrs. Robert C. Scull, Great Neck, New York

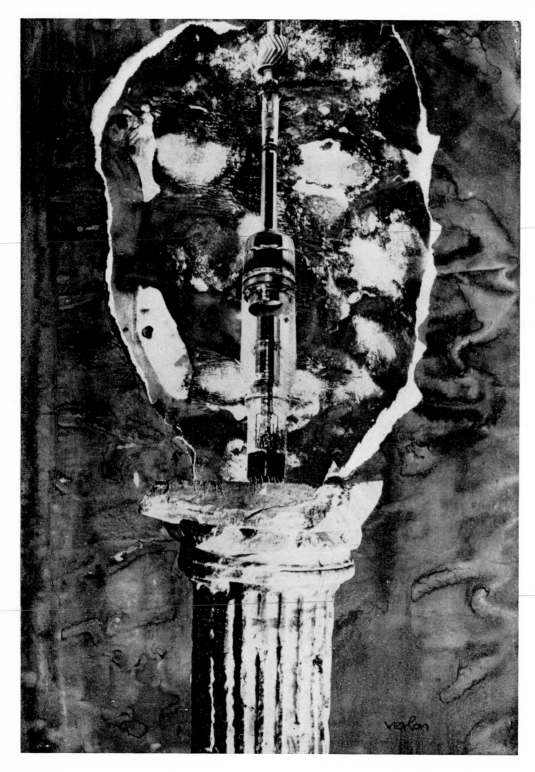

opposite, Verlon: *No Escape?* (1958). Pasted colored photoengravings on paper, with gouache, 16x11″. Willy Verkauf, Vienna

below, Jess: *Nadine.* 1955. Cut and pasted illustrations, window-shade pull, etc., on board, 16½x24½″. Dilexi Gallery, San Francisco

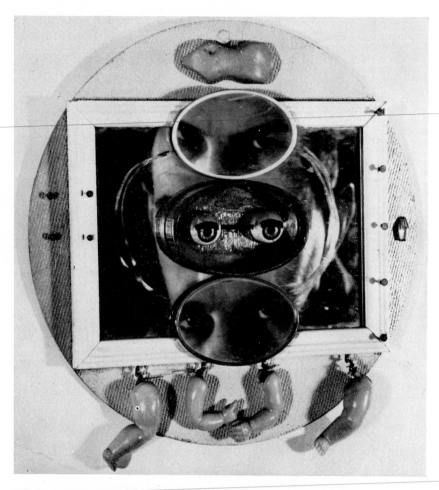

Cohen: *Anybody's Self Portrait*. (1953). Framed mirror mounted on masonite, 9⅝″ diameter, with other objects. Richard Feigen Gallery, Chicago

opposite, Baj: *Mirror*. 1959. Broken mirror glass on brocade fabric, 33⅛x23⅜″. Galleria Schwarz, Milan

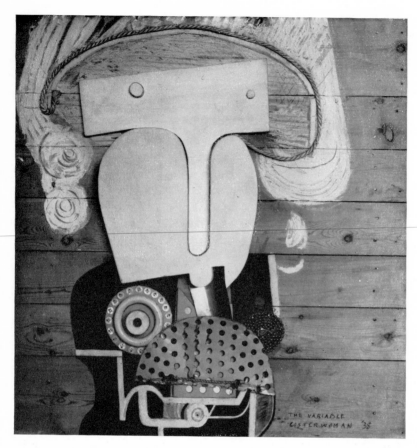

Richards: *The Variable Costerwoman*. 1938. Wood, metal, pearl buttons, etc., 30¼x29¼". Owned by the artist

below, Dominguez: *Happy New Year*. (1954). Sheet brass and sardine can keys, 9¼x13¼", mounted over paper on plywood, 15¾x19¼". Galleria Schwarz, Milan

Nesch: *The Snorer.* (1942-43). Wood, corks, etc., on plywood, 30⅝x41½″. Owned by the artist

Painting relates to both art and life. Neither can be made. (I try to act in that gap between the two.)

I am trying to check my habits of seeing, to counter them for the sake of greater freshness. I am trying to be unfamiliar with what I'm doing.

If you do not change your mind about something when you confront a picture you have not seen before, you are either a stubborn fool or the painting is not very good.

ROBERT RAUSCHENBERG

There is no more subject in a combine *than there is in a page from a newspaper. Each thing that is there is a subject. It is a situation involving multiplicity. (It is no reflection on the weather that such and such a government sent a note to another.)*

Would we have preferred a pig with an apple in its mouth? That too, on occasion, is a message and requires a blessing. These are the feelings Rauschenberg gives us: love, wonder, laughter, heroism (I accept), fear, sorrow, anger, disgust, tranquillity.

Perhaps after all there is no message. In that case one is saved the trouble of having to reply. As the lady said, "Well, if it isn't art, then I like it." Some (a) were made to hang on a wall, others (b) to be in a room, still others (a + b).

JOHN CAGE
All above quotations from John Cage, "On Rauschenberg, Artist, and His Work," Metro, vol. 1, no. 2, 1961, pp. 36-50

Rauschenberg: *Talisman.* (1958). "Combine-painting" of oil paint, paper, wood, etc., 42x28″. Collection Mr. and Mrs. Arnold H. Maremont, Chicago

opposite, Rauschenberg: *Canyon.* 1959. "Combine-painting" of oil on canvas, with wood, printed matter, stuffed eagle, pillow tied with cord, etc., 6′1″ high x 5′6″ wide x 24¾″ deep. Collection Mr. and Mrs. Michael Sonnabend, New York

Louise Nevelson is an inveterate collector of found objects. In the living quarters of her many-chambered atelier on the lower east side of New York, odd and fascinating discoveries lie casually on shelves and tables. Clustered on the walls, to be admired, are finely polished and beautifully worn old tools and utensils. But she does not incorporate such objects, already complete and expressive, in sculpture. Neatly categorized and stacked in the storerooms and work spaces on the lower floors, which Nevelson commands like a modern Rubens, are her materials: boxes of many shapes and sizes, newel posts, the arms, seats, splats and backs of chairs, legs from many kinds of tables, wooden disks and cylinders, balusters and finials, chunks of natural wood and, from the lumber yard, lengths of patterned molding, acanthus scrolls, and clean boards. Uninteresting in themselves yet fragments with a form and history, these are the elements of her sculpture.

"Assemblage," is "the fitting together of parts and pieces." What an instinctive, even compulsive, assembler Louise Nevelson is! And her sculptural and poetic judgment is unerring. Each gilt-sprayed compartment of Royal Tide I is complete, and absolute in its clarity, yet each functions as a unit in a poem of eighteen stanzas. Those qualities that Schwitters loved — traces of human use, weather, and forgotten craftsmanship — still exert their magic here, but their color and dispersiveness is formalized by the gilding. Depth is flattened, but the reflecting surfaces delineate each block, sphere or volute, dowel hole, slot or recess, with scholastic thoroughness and precision.

This authoritative work resembles a reredos, an altar; but its dedication is not to a spiritualized divinity. The immediacy, clarity, and tangibility of its form and surface muffle and control, though they do not obliterate, an atmosphere of mysticism and romanticism. The gold is as much that of Versailles as of Burgos.

Nevelson: *Royal Tide I.* 1960. Gilded wood, 8′ high x 3′ wide. Martha Jackson Gallery, New York

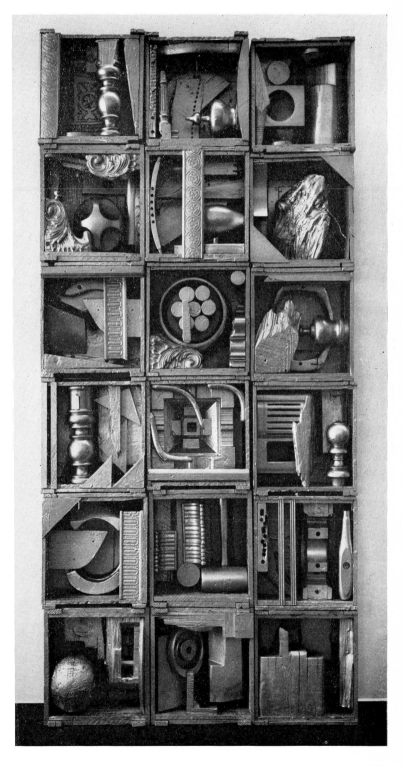

Simon: *Kiosk*. (1961). Construction of wood and maple-wood type, 36½″ high x 24″ wide. Owned by the artist

Bouras: *The D's Testament*. 1961. Wood, steel, plumbing fixtures, etc., 36x48″. Collection Mr. and Mrs. James M. Alter, Chicago

. . . it is perfectly legitimate to use numbers and printed letters as pictorial elements; new in art, they are already soaked with humanity.

GUILLAUME APOLLINAIRE [99]

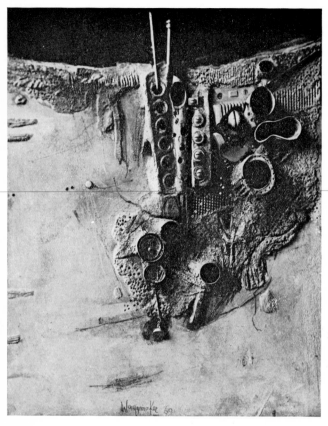

Wagemaker: *Metallic Grey*. 1960. Oil, aluminum egg slicer and other hardware, etc., on board 24x19¾″. Owned by the artist

de Saint-Phalle: *Tu est moi*. 1960. Steel gear, toy pistol, rope, and other objects, on painted plywood, 31½x23⅝″. Private collection, New York

One of the images that Mallarmé used to define books was a butterfly (*pages as wings, spine as body*). John Latham's books, cut, torn, and burned, resemble moths in their symmetry, in the crisp, soft furry pages, and in their ashen, somewhat lunar, complexion. . . . Latham's libraries (*my word for his work-in-progress*), on the other hand, render mass-produced objects unique. Duchamp in his Unhappy Readymade *exposed a geometry book to the weather. Latham does something of the sort, except that he keeps the process of transformation in his own hands. He destroys the function of books as records of verbal information. This is a loaded gesture in a culture like ours in which libraries are repositories of 'the wisdom of the ages' and in which books are used by the heaviest readers as bricks to build walls against the barbarians of visual mass culture. But Latham's destructive gesture turns into an act of creation, as non-verbal art appears out of the wreckage of the printed word. The effacement of the known code is related to the emergence of a previously unknown object. The versatility of objects when subjected to disinterested acts of esthetic decision, allows Latham to play with both the original status and the transformation of his books.*

LAWRENCE ALLOWAY
From an exhibition catalogue, Institute of Contemporary Arts, London, 1960

Latham: *Shem.* 1958. Hessian-covered door, with books and other objects, 8′4″x4′. Owned by the artist

Follett: Untitled. (1958). Iron and steel hardware, mirror, rope, etc., on wood, 24x30″. Green Gallery, New York

Hirscher: *Straits of Magellan*. 1960. Driftwood, metal, crushed tin can, fabric, paper, etc., 25¼x15″. Owned by the artist

below, Schloss: *Dow Road*. 1958. Box of weathered wood, with torn printed page and wallpaper, lace, glass bottle, etc., 13″ high x 9″ wide x4½″ deep. Owned by artist

Arman: *Little Hands (Ainsi font, font . . .)* 1960. Dolls' hands glued in wooden drawer, 14⅝" high x 17⅞" wide x 2⅞" deep. Collection **Mr.** and Mrs. Robert C. Scull, Great Neck, New York

opposite, Fièvre: *The Guardians.* 1961. Wood compartments, with **driftwood,** stones, snakeskin, etc., 35½x15¾". Galerie Daniel Cordier, Paris

Goeritz: *Message No. 14.* "*And thy heaven that is over thy head shall be brass, and the earth that is under thee shall be iron.*" Deuteronomy 28:23. 1959. Metal and paint on painted wood, 28¼x22". Carstairs Gallery, New York

opposite, Conner: *Deadly Nightshade.* 1959. Wooden window frame with glass, containing miscellaneous materials and objects, 43½x33½". Collection Dr. Arthur J. Neumann, Chicago

Smith: *Paul's Wood Bob*. (1956). Welded steel rings on steel plate, 10¾x12″. Everett Ellin Gallery, Los Angeles

opposite, Coetzee: *Butterfly Lighting in a Diamond*. (1960). Oil on canvas, bicycle parts, etc., 6′4½″x52″. Collection Philip C. Johnson, New Canaan, Connecticut

Spoerri: *Kichka's Breakfast.* 1960. Wooden chair, with utensils and remains of two breakfasts, 14⅜″ high x 27¼″ wide x 25¼″ deep. Galleria Schwarz, Milan

Daniel Spoerri is not a painter; however, his snare pictures make one think of the still lifes they could inspire. Spoerri doesn't pretend to create works of art, nor does he proclaim that his works exalt non-art or anti-art. The emotion that they release is not of the same order as that aroused by painting or sculpture; on the other hand, this emotion resembles in no way that brought about by the same objects before Spoerri has glued them and placed them vertically. His snare pictures are situated at the intersection of art and life, at the point where contradictions cancel one another out.

. . . Spoerri condemns us to contemplate the remains of a breakfast, just as a director forces us, by means of the close-up, to become conscious of the evocative power of objects. But perhaps the most frightening thing about these snare pictures is their permanence, their

stability. "Why should my snare pictures produce a malaise?" writes Spoerri. "Because I detest immobility, I detest everything that is settled. The contradiction that exists in the fact that I affix objects, cut them off from the possibility of continual movement and trans-formation, though I love movement and change, pleases me. I love contradictions because they create tension." Indeed, that Spoerri snares these accidental situations, retires them from their uncertain destiny in the course of daily life, and ejects them, so to speak, into the timeless world of art, is what gives rise to the feeling of exasperation with which one looks at a snare picture. . . .

ALAIN JOUFFROY
From an exhibition catalogue, Galleria Schwarz, Milan, March, 1961

132

Herms: *Poet*. (1960). Wood, stack of pages tied with string, rusted klaxon, wire, 27″ high.
Collection Dr. Arthur J. Neumann, Chicago

Kienholz: left, *John Doe*. (1959). Mannequin in child's perambulator, oil paint, wood, metal, plaster, 41″ high x 19″ wide x 34″ deep; right, *Jane Doe*. (1959). Wooden sewing chest, head and neck of mannequin, skirt of white bridal dress, oil paint, 42″ high x 27″ wide x 16″ deep. Both, Ferus Gallery, Los Angeles

Marisol: *From France*. 1960. Wood construction beam with painted and stenciled wood, carved wood hat forms, plaster castings, and other objects, 54⅜″ high. Owned by artist

Burri: *All Black*. 1956. Vinavil, tempera, rags, on canvas, 59″x8′2¼″. Owned by the artist

But out of a wound beauty is born. At any rate in the case of Burri. For Burri transmutes rubbish into a metaphor for human, bleeding flesh. He vitalizes the dead materials in which he works, makes them live and bleed; then sews up the wounds evocatively and as sensuously as he made them.

What would have remained with the cubists a partial intensification of a painted composition — with the dadaists, a protest — with the surrealists, an illustrational fantasy — with Kurt Schwitters, a Merzbild — becomes with Burri a living organism: flesh and blood. The representation of the human form in keeping with the trend of our times may not appear in his pictures; but a suggestion of what gave that form life still remains — a suggestion of flesh and blood; and, more important still, a deep sense of order which relates the human form to a higher level of things, the spiritual. From Burri's art only the superficial resemblance to living creatures is absent.

Collage with Burri has taken on another dimension. It is no longer a primarily compositional activity, a jeu d'esprit or a gesture; he has given it a living quality, a sensuous character. Within the limits of his medium he taps the sources of enjoyment Rembrandt drank from so deeply in his Flayed Beef, *Rubens in the flesh of his nudes, Géricault in his corpses. At the same time his work shows a sensibility and delicacy of expression in its most successful examples which gives it for our age and in crudest of materials some of the qualities of a Redon pastel or a Renoir rose.*

JAMES JOHNSON SWEENEY
*From Burri, Rome, Obelisco Galleria d'Arte, 1955,
pp. 5-6*

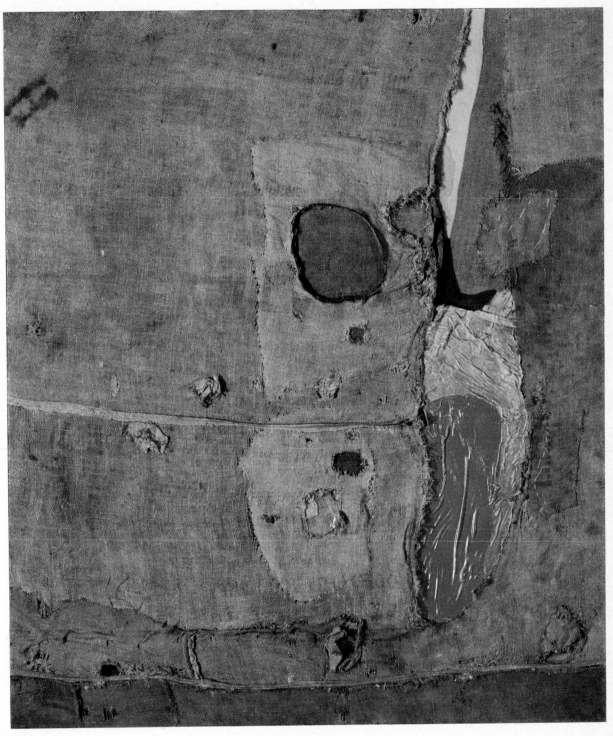

Burri: *Sack Number 5*. (1953). Vinavil and tempera on burlap, 51x50″. Owned by the artist

Chamberlain: *Essex*. (1960). Painted metal, 9' high x 7'6'' wide. Leo Castelli, New York

Bontecou: Untitled. (1960). Construction of steel, canvas, cloth, and wire, 6' high x 56" wide x 20" deep.
Collection Mr. and Mrs. Robert C. Scull, Great Neck, New York

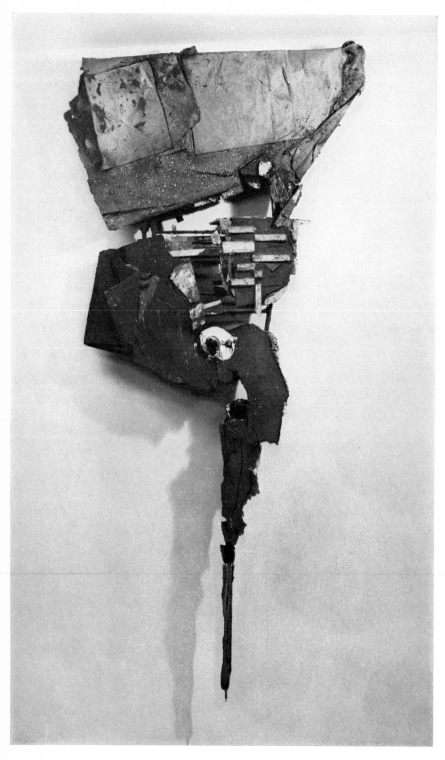

Mallary: *Jouster*. 1960. Wood, steel, paper, etc.
8'5½" high x 49¾" wide. The Allan Stone Gallery,
New York

Indiana: *Moon*. 1960. Wood beam, iron and wood wheels, 7′ high. David Anderson Gallery, New York

Baxter: *Instruments at the Silence Refinery*. (1960). Driftwood, shells, stones, metal, etc., 16″ high x 20″ long. David Cole Gallery, Sausalito, California

Beynon: *Object-Painting Number 37*. 1960. Wood, metal, nylon, sand, plastic, etc., 5'x8'4''. Galerie Stadler, Paris

The sculpture of Richard Stankiewicz is welded together from junk: scrap iron, pieces of discarded machinery, and broken castings. It is to sculpture what the collages of Schwitters, glued together from transfers, tickets, wrappings, and pieces of advertisements are to painting. As Wallace Stevens in The Man on the Dump associates nouns and adjectives one would not naturally associate, so Stankiewicz associates a spring, a weight, and the casting from the top of a gas cooking stove to make a non-machine frozen into immobility by its own rust. "Where was it one first heard of the truth?" Stankiewicz' creativeness is childish and barbaric. He uses things for purposes that were not intended, or only partly so, as the early Christians used pieces of temples for their basilicas, or as a child makes wheels for his cart out of crayons. The original material still shows. Respect for the material is common enough in art; it is part of the organic theory. But his material has already been used once and it retains the quality of some previous construction, which was mechanical and functional. . . .

His sculpture, using junk, is a creation of life out of death, the new life being of a quite different nature than the old one that was decaying on the junk pile, on the sidewalk, in the used-car lot. In its decay there is already a new beginning before Stankiewicz gets hold of it. At his best he makes one aware of a vitality that is extra-artistic. His respect for the material is not a machinist's respect, but the respect of someone who can take a machine or leave it, who respects even the life of things, which is more than mechanical.

FAIRFIELD PORTER
From School of New York, *ed. B. H. Friedman,
New York, Grove Press, 1959, pp. 72 and 76*

Stankiewicz: Untitled. (1961). Welded scrap steel parts, 67"⅛ high. Collection Mr. and Mrs. Burton G. Tremaine, The Miller Company, Meridan, Connecticut

César peering through a stack of compressed scrap automobile bodies.

César: *Motor 4.* (1960). Welded metal, 16″ high x 21″ long. Saidenberg Gallery, New York

. . . In a factory for the salvaging of metals in the suburbs of Paris I saw César in front of one of the latest American compressors, supervising the movements of the cranes, proportioning the heterogeneous loads, eagerly awaiting the result of each operation. Together we admired these calibrated bales weighing nearly a ton which are the product of the compression of a small lorry, a pile of bicycles or of a gigantic set of kitchen stoves.

. . . César sees in the result of this mechanical compression a new stage of metal, one subjected, so to speak, to a quintessential reduction. . . .

. . . For beyond the American neo-dadaist provocations his oeuvre opens one of the roads to the new realism; it is high time that the public recognized that this realism is the essential achievement of this second half-century.

Pierre Restany
From an exhibition catalogue, Hanover Gallery, London, 1960

145

above, Jacobsen: *Head with Keys*. (1957). Iron, 31″ high. Collection Mr. and Mrs. Arnold H. Maremont, Chicago

above right, Tajiri: *Samurai*. (1960). Welded metal parts, nuts and bolts, 33½″ high. Owned by the artist

right, Jacobs: *Ursula*. (1960). Welded machine parts, 19″ high. Barone Gallery, New York

Seley: *Masculine Presence*. (1961). Welded automobile bumpers, grill, 7′8″ high x 4′ wide. Barone Gallery, New York

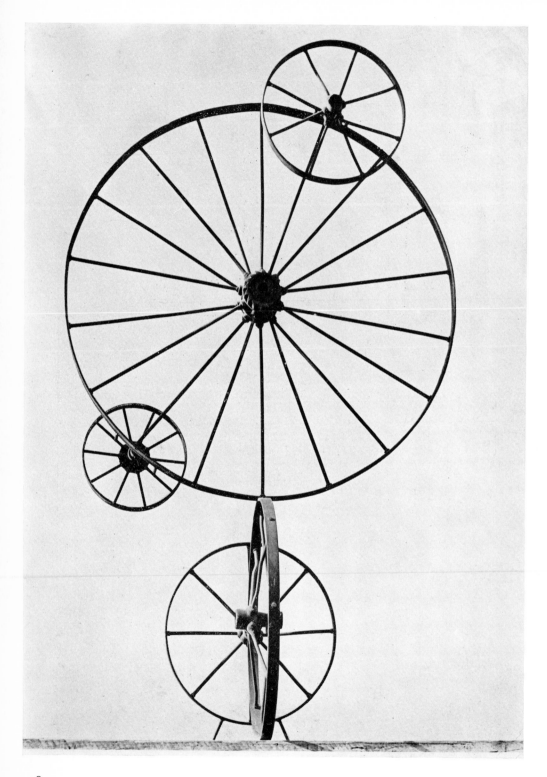

Colla . . . confines himself to used, worn, or old parts, so that his totemic figures and marked reliefs never emerge from a single stock of material (as Gonzalez's or Smith's do) but bind together forms of widely-separated origins. The difference in Colla's attitude towards materials arises from his attachment to the object with a history (and this is no less true of his work in wood). Here Colla has contact with the Dadaists who discovered the plastic vitality of banal objects and, as a result, brought into aesthetics a world of common artifacts. Removed from its familiar utilitarian context and put into an aesthetic situation the found object prospered. Colla subjects the found object to a rigorous processing, very different from the polemical work of Duchamp and Picabia. Colla is separated from other iron sculptors by his exclusive use of found objects and he is separated from Dada by the formality of his work, the result of meditation, not of ambushing habit (as with the early Dadaists).

LAWRENCE ALLOWAY
From Ettore Colla: Iron Sculpture,
Rome, Grafica, 1960 [p. 11]

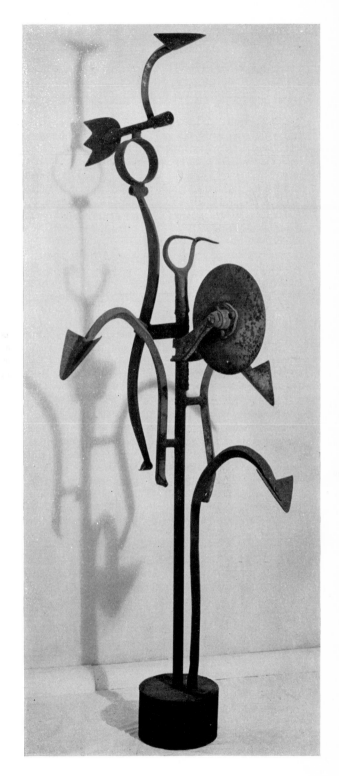

Colla: *Agreste.* (1952). Welded parts of farm implements, 7′4⅜″ high x 31½″ wide. Owned by the artist

opposite, Colla: *Continuity.* (1951). Welded construction of wheels, 7′11⅛″ high x 53″ wide. Owned by the artist

NOTES

1 See page 48.

2 Max Ernst, *Beyond Painting*, New York, Wittenborn, Schultz, 1948, p. 22.

3 Alfred H. Barr, Jr., *Picasso: Fifty Years of His Art*, New York, The Museum of Modern Art, 1946, p. 79.

4 *Loc. cit.* Picasso's *Notre avenir est dans l'air* (Zervos vol. 2, pt. 2, p. 321) is very close to the *Still Life with Chair Caning* in form.

5 The French word *collage*, after the verb *coller*, means "pasting, sticking, or gluing," as in the application of wallpaper. As a method of picture-making used by modern artists, its "invention" is credited to Picasso, and that of *papier collé*, or pasted paper, to Braque in his *Compotier et verre*, September 1912. (See Douglas Cooper, *G. Braque* (exhibition catalogue), Arts Council of Great Britain, 1956, p. 35.) John Golding, *Cubism: A History and an Analysis, 1907-1914*, New York, Wittenborn, 1959, pp. 102 ff., gives a detailed account of the beginnings of modern collage and the addition of such extraneous materials as oilcloth, mirrors, postage stamps, etc., to paintings and drawings. Golding notes (p. 104) that collage was first discussed in print by Maurice Raynal in the *Section d'Or*, a periodical that appeared (for one issue) in connection with the cubist exhibition of 1912.

Little can be said to distinguish the terms *collage* and *papier collé* except that the latter is narrower both technically and historically, referring only to paper and (in the usage I prefer, at least) to paper collages of the cubist movement. (See entries in the *Encyclopaedia of the Arts*, New York, Philosophical Library, 1946, and the *Dictionary of Modern Painting*, New York, Tudor, [1955].

It is, of course, an error to say that the cubists invented pasting as a method of picture-making. Dates for its origin can be pushed backward endlessly. Alfred Barr has called my attention to a drawing by Picasso of 1908 (Zervos, *Picasso*, vol. 2, pt. 1, p. 34) which includes a fragment of pasted paper, probably to make a correction. Penrose notes that Picasso's father used cutouts on his canvases (as de Kooning did for his "Women") to try out new ideas (*Picasso: His Life and Work*, London, Victor Gollancz, and New York, Harper, 1958, p. 171). Valentines, postcards, and folk art of various kinds incorporating pasted elements, as well as pictures and objects made of butterfly wings, feathers, shells, etc., were common much earlier. Indeed, variously stamped letters, passports, and official documents can be looked at as a form of unintentional collage. Herta Wescher (*Art Aujourd'hui*, vol. 5, no. I, Feb. 1954, p. 3) illustrates a Japanese *papier collé*, used as a background for calligraphy, of the tenth century.

As Jean Dubuffet realized in 1953, the term collage is not broad enough to cover the diversity of modern composite art. "Il m'a semblé," he wrote to me in a letter of April 21, 1961," que le mot 'collages' ne devait pas être considéré comme un terme générique désignant n'importe quel ouvrage ou intervient de la colle, mais comme un terme historique réservé aux collages faits dans la période 1910/1920 par les dadaïstes, Picasso et Braque, etc. Ces travaux participaient d'une certaine 'humeur' qui me semble liée au mot, tout aussi bien que le mot 'symboliste' est lié à un certain climat d'époque et provoquerait des malentendus si on le réemployait pour des poèmes faits dans un autre temps quand bien même ceux-ci feraient usage de symboles."

The term "assemblage," used by Dubuffet (see page 93), was adopted for this book and exhibition out of necessity, as a generic concept that would include all forms of composite art and modes of juxtaposition. In both French and English "assemblage" denotes "the fitting together of parts and pieces," and can apply to both flat and three-dimensional forms. Both as verb and noun, moreover, this word repeatedly occurs in the literature of modern art. Certain of the two-dimensional modes and methods it denotes follow:

Décollage is the opposite of collage: "ungluing," "unsticking," or "taking off." It refers to works made by removing materials already pasted, as in the *décollages* of Austin Cooper or Gwyther Irwin, and the *affiches lacerées*, or torn posters, of the Parisian "new realists." *Découpage* (literally "cutting") is a mode of decorating painted furniture with cutouts of flowers, fruit, etc., but the term is also used to denote cleanly cut collage of new paper (not considered in this book) such as that of Matisse, Taeuber-Arp, Sonia Delaunay, *et al.*

"Photomontage" (assemblages of photographs made by pasting or other means) has been practiced, both for practical reasons and as "trick photography" since at least the middle of the nineteenth century. The term gained its present meaning through its use by the German dadas for collages of photographs and other illustrative material, beginning before 1920. With an ironic intent, they appropriated the German verb *montieren*, a synonym of our verb "to assemble," and applied, as in one of our usages, to the mounting and erection of machinery. The dadas' expansion of this meaning survives not only in the common term "photomontage," but also in the application of the term "montage" to the film. (For a lucid discussion of montage see Sergei Eisenstein, *The Film Sense*, New York, Harcourt, Brace, 1942. For the dada use of photomontage, John Heartfield, *Photomontagen zur Zeitgeschichte*, Zurich, Kultur und Vol, 1945.)

6 Barr, *op. cit.*, p. 87.

7 See note no. 5.

8 See Alan Bowness, "A note on 'Manet's Compositional Difficulties,'" *The Burlington Magazine*, vol. 103, no. 699, Jan. 1961, pp. 276-277.

9 See George Heard Hamilton, *Manet and his Critics*, New Haven, Yale University Press, 1954, p. 115.

10 Roger Fry, *Cézanne: A Study of his Development*, London, Leonard and Virginia Woolf, Hogarth Press, 1927, p. 47.

11 The term *Gestalt* (literally "form," "shape," or "figure"), used in Germany by Charles von Ehrenfels ca. 1890, was the basis for a school of psychology, of which Koffka and Köhler became the leading spokesmen, which asserts that a whole is greater than the sum of its parts, and that each element in a given pattern is altered by its participation in a relational unity.

12 Robert Goldwater and Marco Treves, *Artists on Art*, New York, Pantheon, 1945, p. 375.

13 See Marcel Jean, *The History of Surrealist Painting*, New York, Grove Press, 1960, p. 12.

14 Roger Fry, tr., *The Poems of Mallarmé*, New York, New Directions, 1951, p. 290.

15 Wallace Fowlie, *A Guide to Contemporary French Literature*, New York, Meridian, 1957, p. 100.

16 Charles Mauron, in Fry, *Mallarmé*, p. 284.

17 *Ibid.*, p. 300.

18 *Ibid.*, p. 301.

19 Roger Shattuck, *The Banquet Years*, New York, Harcourt Brace, 1958, p. 259.

20 Guillaume Apollinaire, *The Cubist Painters*, New York, Wittenborn, Schultz, 2nd ed., 1949, p. 23.

21 Shattuck, *op. cit.*, p. 245.

22 *Ibid.*, p. 215.

23 As Eisenstein and others have pointed out, montage is essential to film technique. It is interesting to note Eisenstein regarded over-dependence on montage as a sort of left-wing deviation. These "leftists" of montage, he felt, were naïvely wrapped up in the fact that (as he writes in italics on page 4 of *The Film Sense*) *"two film pieces of any kind, placed together, inevitably combine into a new concept, a new quality, arising out of that juxtaposition.* . . . This is not in the least a circumstance peculiar to the cinema," he goes on to say in the next paragraph, "but is a phenomenon invariably met with in all cases where we have to deal with juxtaposition of two facts, two phenomena, two objects." The aims of "socialist realism" inhibited a full liberation of images, but Eisenstein's analysis of montage and juxtaposition (according to Gestalt principles) is nevertheless of interest in the present context.

24 *Lundi Rue Christine* first appeared in *Soirées de Paris*, vol. 2, no. 19, Dec. 15, 1913, p. 27.

Three lit gas jets
The proprietress has lung trouble
When you've finished we'll have a game of backgammon
An orchestra conductor who has a sore throat
When you come to Tunis I'll have you smoke some kiff

This seems to rhyme

25 Cecily Mackworth, *Guillaume Apollinaire and the Cubist Life*, London, John Murray, 1961, pp. 150-151.

26 Shattuck, *op. cit.*, p. 238.

27 See *Les Mots en Liberté Futuristes*, Milan, Poesia, 1919.

28 André Gide, *The Counterfeiters: with Journal of "The Counterfeiters,"* New York, Knopf, 1959, p. 406, a journal entry of Jan. 3, 1924.

29 *Ibid.*, p. 174.

30 Wylie Sypher, *Rococo to Cubism in Art and Literature*, New York, Random House, 1960, p. 308.

31 Guillaume Apollinaire, *Les Peintres Cubistes*, Paris, Figuière, 1913, pp. 35-36.

32 Daniel-Henry Kahnweiler, *The Rise of Cubism*, New York, Wittenborn, Schultz, 1949, p. 1. A translation of *Der Weg zum Kubismus*, Munich, Delphin, 1920.

33 Piet Mondrian, *Plastic Art and Pure Plastic Art*, New York, Wittenborn, 1945, p. 38.

34 Kahnweiler, *Juan Gris: His Life and Work*, New York, Valentin, 1947, p. 117.

35 *Ibid.*, p. 88, and f.n.

36 *Violon et cruche*, Kunstmuseum, Basel. See Golding, *op. cit.*, pl. 28, and Robert Rosenblum, *Cubism and Twentieth Century Art*, New York, Abrams, 1960, pl. IX.

37 Kahnweiler, *Juan Gris*, pp. 87-88. He speaks of *The Dressing Table* (*Le Lavabo*). See also Golding, *op. cit.*, p. 102. Gris uses a mirror also in *The Marble Console* (1914) in the Maremont Collection, Chicago.

38 *Ibid.*, p. 86.

39 *Ibid.*, p. 88.

40 *Ibid.*, p. 86.

41 Shattuck, *op. cit.*, p. 256.

42 *Initial Manifesto of Futurism.* See Joshua C. Taylor, *Futurism*, New York, The Museum of Modern Art, 1961, p. 124.

43 Tr. from an interview in *Arts* (Paris), May 10, 1961, p. 18.

44 See Taylor, *op. cit.*, p. 132.

45 See exhibition catalogue, *Salute to Italy: One Hundred Years of Italian Art*, Hartford, Wadsworth Atheneum, 1961.

46 See Taylor, *op. cit.*, f.n. 32, p. 120; and Gino Severini, *Tutta la Vita*, p. 175.

47 Carrieri dates this work 1911; Taylor, *ibid.*, p. 93, 1912. See also notes 43, 45, 48, 49, p. 120; and "Chronology," p. 122.

48 *Ibid.*, p. 126.

49 *Loc. cit.*

50 *Ibid.*, p. 127.

51 *Ibid.*, p. 129.

52 Written for *The Dada Painters and Poets*, Robert Motherwell, ed., New York, Wittenborn, Schultz, 1951, but printed as a separate sheet because of a disagreement between Huelsenbeck and Tzara.

53 In "What Abstract Art Means to Me," *The Museum of Modern Art Bulletin*, vol. 18, no. 3, Spring, 1951, p. 7.

54 Quoted by Georges Lemaitre, *From Cubism to Surrealism in French Literature*, Cambridge, Mass., Harvard, 1947, p. 169.

55 Motherwell, *op. cit.*, p. 78.

56 *DADA 1916-1923*, New York (exhibition catalogue, Sidney Janis Gallery), 1953.

57 Jean, *op. cit.*, p. 124.

58 *Ibid.*, p. 39.

59 *Ibid.*, p. 47.

60 *Ibid.*, p. 41.

61 *Ibid.*, p. 40.

62 James Thrall Soby, *Giorgio de Chirico*, New York, The Museum of Modern Art, 1955, p. 66.

63 ". . . beau . . . comme la rencontre fortuite sur une table de dissection d'une machine à coudre et d'un parapluie!" Le Comte de Lautréamont (Isadore Ducasse), *Les Chants de Maldoror*, Paris, Brussels, n. publ., 1874, pp. 289-290.

64 Alfred H. Barr, Jr., *Fantastic Art, Dada, Surrealism*, New York, The Museum of Modern Art, 1936, p. 45.

65 Max Ernst, *Beyond Painting*, New York, Wittenborn, Schultz, 1948, p. 21.

66 *Loc. cit.*

67 See *The Bride Stripped Bare by Her Bachelors, Even*, New York, Wittenborn, 1960, n.p.

68 Robert Lebel, *Marcel Duchamp*, New York, Grove Press, 1959, p. 45.

69 Kate Steinitz, *The Merzbau of Kurt Schwitters*, unpublished ms., Los Angeles, n. d.

70 Robert Motherwell, *The School of New York*, Beverly Hills (exhibition catalogue, Frank Perls Gallery), 1951.

71 In *Architectural Design*, (London), vol. 31, no. 3, March 1961, p. 122.

72 Shattuck, *op. cit.*, p. 228.

73 Reyner Banham, in *Arts*, vol. 35, no. 3, Dec. 1960, p. 35.

74 Foreword for the catalogue of a Marin exhibition at Stieglitz' "291" Gallery, New York 1912. See Mackinley Helm, *John Marin*, Boston, Pellegrini & Cudahy, [1948], p. 28.

75 Thomas B. Hess, "De Kooning Paints a Picture," *Art News*, vol. 52, no. 1, March 1953, p. 31.

76 By Friedrich (Fritz) Hundertwasser. See *Arts*, vol. 33, no. 5, Feb. 1959, p. 36.

77 From "Rhapsody on a Windy Night," 1917, in *Collected Poems 1909-1935*, New York, Harcourt, Brace & World, 1936.

78 Jean, *op. cit.*, p. 66.

79 Barr, *Picasso*, p. 270.

80 Kahnweiler, *Juan Gris*, p. 138.

81 From a catalogue of a Spoerri exhibition, Milan, Galleria Schwarz, 1961. See also p. 132.

82 *Loc. cit.*

83 In an unpublished ms., Paris, 1961.

84 Quoted by Shattuck, *op. cit.*, p. 264.

85 Apollinaire, *op. cit.*, p. 21.

86 Marcel Duchamp, "The Creative Act," in Lebel, *op. cit.*, pp. 77-78.

87 Banham, *op. cit.*, p. 37.

88 André Gide, *op. cit.*, p. 396.

89 Allen Kaprow, *Paintings, Environments, and Happenings*, (ms. scheduled for publication in the near future), Old Bridge, N. J., 1960.

90 Quoted by Basil Taylor, "Art — Anti-Art," *The Listener*, (London), Nov. 12, 1959, p. 281.

91 See Jasia Reichhardt, "Expendable Art," *Architectural Design* (London), vol. 30, no. 10, Oct. 1960, p. 421. Jean Tinguely's *Homage to New York* also discussed.

92 *Loc. cit.*

93 Basil Taylor, *op. cit.*, p. 819.

94 Kaprow, *op. cit.*, p. 12a.

95 *Ibid.*, p. 12.

96 Jill Johnson, in *Art News*, vol. 60, no. 2, April 1961, p. 57.

97 Gide, *op. cit.*, p. 415.

98 Robert Motherwell, from "Beyond the Aesthetic," *Design*, vol. 47, no. 8, April 1946, pp. 14-15.

99 Apollinaire, *op. cit.*, p. 21.

PHOTOGRAPH CREDITS

CATALOGUE OF THE EXHIBITION

LENDERS

Mr. and Mrs. Eddie Albert, Pacific Palisades, California; Mr. and Mrs. James W. Alsdorf, Winnetka, Illinois; Mr. and Mrs. James M. Alter, Chicago; Mr. and Mrs. E. A. Bergman, Chicago; Victor Brauner, Paris; George Brecht, Metuchen, New Jersey; Mr. and Mrs. Leonard Brown, Springfield, Massachusetts; Camille Bryen, Paris; Mrs. Edith Schloss Burckhardt, New York; Alberto Burri, Rome; Mrs. Gilbert W. Chapman, New York; Ivan Chermayeff, New York; Ettore Colla, Rome; Carlo Corsi, Bologna; Mme Crotti-Duchamp, Neuilly-sur-Seine; Robyn Denny, London; Miss Sari Dienes, New York; Samuel Dubiner, Tel Aviv; Miss Marisol Escobar, New York; Mr. and Mrs. Solomon Ethe, New York; Whitney Halstead, Chicago; Heinz E. Hirscher, Stuttgart; Frau Hannah Höch, Berlin; Marcel Jean, Paris; Philip C. Johnson, New Canaan, Connecticut; Dr. and Mrs. Hans J. Kleinschmidt, New York; Mr. and Mrs. Samuel M. Kootz, New York; Mrs. Katharine Kuh, New York; John Latham, London; Miss Elizabeth McFadden, New York; Mr. and Mrs. Arnold H. Maremont, Chicago; Mrs. Pierre Matisse, New York; Mr. and Mrs. Jean de Menil, Houston; N. Richard Miller, New York; Robert Motherwell, New York; H. Marc Moyens, Alexandria, Virginia; Rolf Nesch, Aal, Norway; Dr. Arthur J. Neumann, Chicago; Mr. and Mrs. Morton G. Neumann, Chicago; Robert Nickle, Chicago; Eduardo Paolozzi, London; Roland Penrose, London; Marvin Preston, West Ferndale, Michigan; Robert Rauschenberg, New York; Man Ray, Paris; Mr. and Mrs. Bernard J. Reis, New York; Mr. and Mrs. John Rewald, New York; Ceri Richards, London; Mrs. John D. Rockefeller, 3rd, New York; Nelson A. Rockefeller, New York; Mimmo Rotella, Rome; Mr. and Mrs. Robert C. Scull, Great Neck, New York; Mr. and Mrs. Joseph R. Shapiro, Oak Park, Illinois; Mme Y. Silvers, Paris; Sidney Simon, New City, New York; Mr. and Mrs. Michael Sonnabend, New York; Miss Laura Lee Stearns, Los Angeles; Shinkichi Tajiri, Amsterdam; Mrs. Yves Tanguy, Woodbury, Connecticut; Mr. and Mrs. G. David Thompson, Pittsburgh; Mr. and Mrs. Burton G. Tremaine, The Miller Company, Meridan, Connecticut; Tristan Tzara, Paris; Willy Verkauf, Vienna; Mrs. Eleanor Ward, New York; Jaap Wagemaker, Amsterdam; Mr. and Mrs. William H. Weintraub, New York; Miss Charmion von Wiegand, New York; Mr. and Mrs. Harry Lewis Winston, Birmingham, Michigan; Mr. and Mrs. George Wittenborn, Scarsdale, New York; Richard S. Zeisler, New York.

Stedelijk Museum, Amsterdam; Buffalo Museum of Science, Buffalo, New York; Yale University Art Gallery, New Haven, Connecticut; The Metropolitan Museum of Art, New York; The Museum of Modern Art, New York; Musée de l'Homme, Paris; Philadelphia Museum of Art; Washington University, St. Louis, Missouri; Schenectady Museum Association, Schenectady, New York.

The Alan Gallery, New York; David Anderson Gallery, New York; Barone Gallery, New York; Brook Street Gallery, London; Carstairs Gallery, New York; Leo Castelli, New York; Galerie Iris Clert, Paris; David Cole Gallery, Sausalito, California; Galerie Daniel Cordier, Paris; Dilexi Gallery, San Francisco; The Downtown Gallery, New York; Charles Egan Gallery, New York; Robert Elkon Gallery, New York; Everett Ellin Gallery, Los Angeles; André Emmerich Gallery, New York; Richard Feigen Gallery, Chicago; Ferus Gallery, Los Angeles; Rose Fried Gallery, New York; Allan Frumkin Gallery, New York; Gimpel Fils, London; Graham Gallery, New York; Grand Central Moderns, New York; Green Gallery, New York; Grosvenor Gallery, London; Stephen Hahn Gallery, New York; Galerie J, Paris; Martha Jackson Gallery, New York; Sidney Janis Gallery, New York; Felix Landau Gallery, Los Angeles; Galerie Louise Leiris, Paris; Royal S. Marks, New York; Pierre Matisse Gallery, New York; Tibor de Nagy Gallery, New York; The New Gallery, New York; Betty Parsons Gallery, New York; Galerie Rive Droite, Paris; Saidenberg Gallery, New York; Galleria Schwarz, Milan; Stable Gallery, New York; Galerie Stadler; Paris; Staempfli Gallery, New York; The Allan Stone Gallery, New York, Catharine Viviano Gallery, New York; Zabriskie Gallery, New York.

CATALOGUE

As a record of the types of materials and objects used in assembled art, this catalogue lists them in some detail. Dimensions are in inches, height preceding width. Dates enclosed in parentheses do not appear on the works of art. Information which differs from illustration captions is based on subsequent examination of actual works. Works to be shown at only one or two museums are marked by (NY), (D) or (SF) to indicate New York, Dallas, or San Francisco. Illustrated works are marked with an asterisk.

ANONYMOUS
1 Gargoyle. French, 15th or 16th century. Lead water pipe in the form of an animal, 11¾″ high. Collection Mr. and Mrs. John Rewald, New York.

ANONYMOUS
2 Valentine's card. British, 19th century. Embossed cut "lace" paper, embossed paper figures, lead paper, marbleized paper, ink, cloth flowers, feathers, 9¾x8″. The Metropolitan Museum of Art. Gift of Mrs. Bella C. Landauer.

ANONYMOUS
*3 Two-Headed Dog. Mouth of the Chiloongo River, Cambinda, Africa, 19th century. Carved wood, nails, animal teeth, 11″ high x 22¾″ long. Musée de l'Homme, Paris. Ill. p. 83.

ANONYMOUS

4 Fighting charm. Breast ornament. Taburi, British New Guinea. Modern. Tortoise shell base, mounted on coconut fiber, decorated with boar's tusks, shell, seeds, and feathers, 9¾x10.'' Buffalo Museum of Science, Buffalo, New York

AGAR, Eileen. British, born Buenos Aires, 1901; lives in London

5 *Woman Reading.* (1936). Pasted papers with page from "The March of Man," a chronological record, India ink, pressed leaves, 12½x9''. Brook Street Gallery, London

ARMAN (Fernandez). French, born Nice, 1929; lives in Paris

*6 *Little Hands (Ainsi font, font. . .)* 1960. Dolls' hands glued in wooden drawer, 14⅝'' high x 17⅞'' wide x 2⅞'' deep. Collection Mr. and Mrs. Robert C. Scull, Great Neck, New York. Ill. p. 127

*7 *Arteriosclerosis.* 1961. Forks and spoons in glass-covered box, 18¾'' high x 28⅝'' wide x 3'' deep. Galleria Schwarz, Milan. Ill. p. 84

ARP, Jean (Hans). French, born Strasbourg, 1887; lives in Meudon, near Paris, and Basel and Solduno, Switzerland

*8 *Collage with Squares Arranged According to the Law of Chance.* (1916-17). Pasted papers, 19⅛x13⅝''. The Museum of Modern Art, New York. Purchase. Ill. p. 35

*9 *La Trousse du voyageur.* (1917-20.) Wood construction, 7⅝x13''. Collection Tristan Tzara, Paris. (NY) Ill. p. 37

10 *La Trousse d'un da.* (1920) Painted wood construction, 15x10⅝''. Collection Tristan Tzara, Paris. (NY)

BAADER, Johannes. German, active in Berlin dada movement. 1918-20

11 *The Author in His Home.* (ca. 1920). Collage of pasted photographs on book page, 8½x5¾''. The Museum of Modern Art, New York. Purchase

BAARGELD, J. T. (Alfred Grünewald). German. Active in Cologne dada movement, 1918-20; died in avalanche, 1927

*12 *The Red King.* 1920. Pen and ink on pasted wallpaper, 19⅜x15¼''. The Museum of Modern Art, New York. Purchase. Ill. p. 38

BAJ, Enrico. Italian, born Milan, 1924; lives in Milan

*13 *Mirror.* 1959. Broken mirror glass on brocade fabric, 33⅛x23⅜''. Galleria Schwarz, Milan. Ill. p. 113

*14 *Shouting General.* (1960). Oil on canvas, with brocade, hemp, clock dials, medals, leather cartridge belt, rope, pin cushion, embroidered epaulet, water canteen, 57½x45''. Galleria Schwarz, Milan. Ill. p. 104

BALDACCINI, see César

BAXTER, John. American, born San Francisco, California, 1912; lives in San Francisco

*15 *Instruments at the Silence Refinery.* (1960). Driftwood, shells, stones, steel, iron, brass, bronze, ceramic instruments and hardware, copper screening, 16⅞'' high x 24⅜'' long. David Cole Gallery, Sausalito, California. Ill. p. 141

BEASLEY, Bruce. American, born Los Angeles, California, 1939; lives in Berkeley, California

16 *Tree House.* 1960. Welded segments of cast-iron sewer pipe, 20'' high. Everett Ellin Gallery, Los Angeles

BEYNON, Eric. Swiss, born Geneva, 1935; lives in Paris

*17 *Object-Painting Number 37.* 1960. Wood, iron, steel, enamel, wire, chair caning, nylon, sand, plastic, 5'x8'4''. Galerie Stadler, Paris. Ill. p. 142

BONTECOU, Lee. American, born Providence, Rhode Island, 1931; lives in New York

*18 Untitled. (1960). Construction of steel, canvas, cloth and wire, 6' high x 56'' wide x 20'' deep. Collection Mr. and Mrs. Robert C. Scull, Great Neck, New York. Ill. p. 139

BOURAS, Harry. American, born Rochester, New York, 1931; lives in Chicago

*19 *The D's Testament.* 1961. Painted and stenciled wood, steel, plumbing fixtures, bicycle parts, 36'' high x 48'' wide x 5¼'' deep. Collection Mr. and Mrs. James M. Alter, Chicago, Ill. p. 121

BRAQUE, Georges. French, born Argenteuil, 1882; lives in Varengeville (Seine-Inférieure) and Paris

*20 *The Program.* (1913). Pasted playbill, colored paper, facsimile woodgrain, with charcoal and oil on canvas, 25⅝x36¼''. Collection Mr. and Mrs. Bernard J. Reis, New York. Ill. p. 18

*21 *Clarinet.* (1913). Pasted papers, newsprint, facsimile woodgrain, with charcoal, chalk and oil on canvas, 37½x47⅜''. Collection Nelson A. Rockefeller, New York. (NY) Ill. p. 19

BRAUNER, Victor. Romanian, born Piatra-Neamtz, 1903; lives in Paris

*22 *Wolf-Table.* 1939. Wood with parts of stuffed animal, 21⅝'' high x 22⅞'' long x 11'' wide. Owned by the artist. Ill. p. 64

23 *Roy — les contraires trouve l'homme = lire — mélancolie du bien.* 1947. Wax figure, with burr, seeds, pebbles, hair, buckshot, on painted wood, 12¾x6⅝''. Collection Mrs. Katharine Kuh, New York. (NY)

BRECHT, George. American, born New York City, 1926; lives in Metuchen, New Jersey

*24 *Repository.* (1961). Wall cabinet containing pocket watch, tennis ball, thermometer, plastic and rubber handballs, baseball, plastic persimmon, "Liberty" statuette, wooden puzzle, tooth brushes, bottle caps, house number, pencils, preserved worm, pocket mirror, light bulbs, keys, hardware, coins, photographs, playing cards, post card, dollar bill, page from thesaurus, 40⅜'' high x 10½'' wide x 3'' deep. Owned by the artist. Ill. opposite.

BRETON, André. French, born Tinchebray (Orne), 1896; lives in Paris

*25 *Objet-poème.* 1941. Carved wood bust of a man, with keyhole for mouth; wood and metal oil lantern with glass; photograph in metal frame; toy boxing gloves; all mounted on wooden drawing board and black drawing paper, with inscriptions painted in gouache and oil, 18¼'' high x 21⅛'' wide x 4⅜'' deep. Collection Mrs. Yves Tanguy, Woodbury, Connecticut. Ill. p. 67

BRYEN, Camille. French, born Nantes, 1907; lives in Paris

*26 *Objet à fonctionnement: "Morphologie du désir."* (1934-37). Plaster casts of ears mounted on board; black wax candle, flashlight, plywood, 8½'' high x 14½'' wide x 11'' deep. Owned by the artist. Ill. p. 61

BURRI, Alberto. Italian, born Città di Castello, 1915; lives near Rome

*27 *Sack Number 5.* (1953). Vinavil and tempera on burlap and cloth, 51x50''. Owned by the artist. Ill. p. 137

Brecht: *Repository.*
Cat. No. 24

*28 *All Black*. 1956. Vinavil, tempera, rags, on canvas, 59″x8′2¼″ Owned by the artist. Ill. p. 136

CARRÀ, Carlo. Italian, born Quargnento, 1881; lives in Milan
29 *Angle pénétrant de Joffre sur la Marne contre deux cubes allemands*. 1914. Pasted papers, newsprint, postage stamp, pencil, conte crayon, ink, ink wash, 10x13½″. Collection Mr. and Mrs. Harry Lewis Winston, Birmingham, Michigan

CÉSAR (Baldaccini). French, born Marseille, 1921; lives in Paris
*30 *Motor 4*. (1960). Welded steel, iron, copper, nickel pipes, 16″ high x 21″ long. Saidenberg Gallery, New York. Ill. p. 145
31 *The Yellow Buick* (compression). (1961). Collection Mr. and Mrs. John Rewald, New York

CHAMBERLAIN, John. American, born Rochester, Indiana, 1927; lives in New City, New York
32 *Zaar*. (1959). Painted automobile parts and other metal, 44″ high x 78″ long. Collection Mr. and Mrs. Robert C. Scull, Great Neck, New York. (D, SF)
*33 *Essex*. (1960). Painted automobile parts and other metal, 9′ high x 7′6″ wide x 43″ deep. Leo Castelli, New York (NY). Ill. p. 138

CHERMAYEFF, Ivan. American, born London, 1932; lives in New York
34 *Type Collage with Newspaper*. 1957. Torn and pasted 19th-century newspaper and poster, on cardboard, 7x8½″. Owned by the artist.

COETZEE, Christo. South African, born Johannesburg, 1930; lives in Paris
*35 *Butterfly Lighting in a Diamond*. (1960). Oil on canvas, bicycle parts, candlesticks, ping-pong balls, sand, wire, wood, 6′4½″x52″. Collection Philip C. Johnson, New Canaan, Connecticut. Ill. p. 131

COHEN, George. American, born Chicago, 1919; lives in Emerson, Illinois
*36 *Anybody's Self Portrait*. (1953). Framed mirror mounted on painted masonite, 9⅝″ diameter, with mirrors, plastic doll's torso, legs and arms, painted doll's eyes with fiber lashes in tin anchovy can, small metal hand, nail heads, screw eyes, hooks, string, cloth. Richard Feigen Gallery, Chicago. Ill. p. 112
37 *Game Preserve*. (1957). Mirrors, plastic doll's arms, torso, and eyes; metal, with oil paint, mounted on painted wood boards, 12½x 34¼″. Richard Feigen Gallery, Chicago

COLLA, Ettore. Italian, born Parma, 1899; lives in Rome
*38 *Continuity*. (1951). Welded iron wheels from farm machines and pushcarts, 7′11⅛″ high x 53″ wide. Owned by the artist. Ill. p. 148
*39 *Agreste*. (1952). Welded iron and steel farm implements, 7′4⅜″ high x 31½″ wide. Owned by the artist. Ill. p. 149

COLLINS, see Jess

CONNER, Bruce. American, born McPherson, Kansas, 1933; lived until recently in San Francisco
*40 *Deadly Nightshade*. 1959. Wooden window frame with glass; cloth, paper, photograph, cloth belt, cellulose tape, string, tobacco sack, plaster ornament, light pull, wax, paint, and other materials, 43½x33½″. Collection Dr. Arthur J. Neumann, Chicago, Ill. p. 128

Corsi: *Skyscraper*. Cat. No. 58

*41 *Last Supper*. (1961). Wax, rags, silk stocking, hair, electrical wire, tennis balls, nails; applied to top of a wooden table, 38¾″ high x 20″ square. The Alan Gallery, New York. Ill. p. 89

COOPER, Austin. British, born Manitoba, Canada, 1890; lives in London

*42 *Tal-lee*. 1948. Torn and pasted oil and watercolor papers; ink, wax, 14½x22″. Gimpel Fils, London. Ill. p. 102

COPPEL, Jeanne. French, born Galati, Romania, 1896; lives in Paris

43 *Collage*. 1955. Torn and pasted papers on painted burlap, 36¼x 13⅛″. Collection H. Marc Moyens, Alexandria, Virginia

CORNELL, Joseph. American, born New York City, 1903; lives in Flushing, New York. (Boxes are glass-covered unless otherwise noted.)

44 *Taglioni's Jewel Casket*. 1940. Hinged, unglazed wooden box containing glass ice cubes, jewelry, etc., 4¾″ high x 11⅞″ wide x 8¼″ deep. The Museum of Modern Art, New York. Gift of James Thrall Soby

*45 *Medici Slot Machine*. 1942. Compartmented wooden box, with pasted photoengravings and reproductions, glass, compass, wooden cubes, jacks, marbles, counters, 15½″ high x 12″ wide x 4⅜″ deep. Collection Mr. and Mrs. Bernard J. Reis, New York. Ill. p. 69

*46 *Habitat Group for a Shooting Gallery*. 1943. Cabinet containing colored cutouts of parrots; printed cards and papers, dried flowers, feathers, etc., behind shattered glass, 15½″ high x 11⅛″ wide x 4¼″ deep. Ferus Gallery, Los Angeles. (NY). Ill. p. 70

47 *Compartmented Cubes*. (1946-48?). Cabinet containing white wooden cubes in separate compartments, 14″ high x 10⅜″ wide x 2¼″ deep. Collection Mrs. Eleanor Ward, New York

48 *Pink Castle*. (ca. 1948). Wooden box, with engraving, cutout and mounted on wood over mirror-glass, twigs, painted cardboard, and plywood, imitation snow, 10⅛″ high x 16″ wide x 5½″ deep. Collection Mrs. Eleanor Ward, New York

49 *La Favorite*. (ca. 1948). Glass-shelved cabinet covered with sheet music; velvet-covered box; bisque figurine; 10″ high x 8½″ wide x 4½″ deep. Collection Mr. and Mrs. E. A. Bergman, Chicago

50 *Central Park Carrousel — 1950, in Memoriam*. (1950). Construction in wood, mirror, wire netting, and paper, 20¼″ high x 14½″ wide x 6¾″ deep. The Museum of Modern Art, New York. Katharine Cornell Fund

*51 *Apothecary*. 1950. Wooden cabinet with glass jars containing various objects, and liquid and dry materials, in glass compartments, 15⅞″ high x 11⅞″ wide x 4⅝″ deep. Collection Mr. and Mrs. Jean de Menil, Houston, Texas. Ill. p. 71

52 *Dovecote*. (1952). Painted wooden construction with wooden balls, 17x11¾″. Collection Mr. and Mrs. Arnold H. Maremont, Chicago. (NY)

53 *Hôtel Bon Port: Ann in Memory*. 1954. Painted wooden construction with pasted paper, stamps, steel spring, 12¾″ high x 10½″ wide x 3¼″ deep. Collection Mr. and Mrs. E. A. Bergman, Chicago

*54 *Night Skies: Auriga*. (ca. 1954). Box containing painted wooden construction with pasted paper, 19¼″ high x 13½″ wide x 7½″ deep. Collection Mr. and Mrs. E. A. Bergman, Chicago. Ill. p. 71

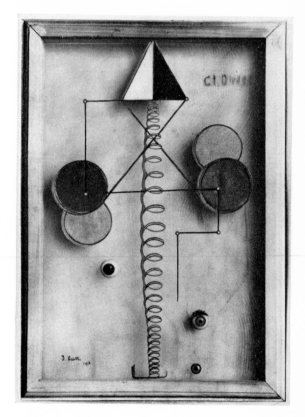

Crotti: *Clown*. Cat. No. 60

55 *Mond-Oberfläche.* (1955). Wooden box containing map, clay pipes, seashell, cordial glass, cork floats on cord, etc., 15⅝x17″. Collection Mr. and Mrs. Arnold H. Maremont, Chicago. (NY)

*56 *Blériot.* (1956). Box containing painted wooden trapeze supported by rusted steel spring, 18½″ high x 11¼″ wide x 4¾″ deep. Collection Mrs. Eleanor Ward, New York. Ill. p. 70

*57 *Space Object Box.* (1959). Wooden construction with painted wood, metal rods and ring, cork ball, cordial glass containing marble, starfish, pasted paper, 9½″ high x 15″ wide x 3¾″ deep. Ferus Gallery, Los Angeles. Ill. p. 68

CORSI, Carlo. Italian, born Nice, France, 1879; lives in Bologna
*58 *Skyscraper.* (1948). Torn and pasted papers, book page, and corrugated cardboard, 15⅞x21″. Owned by the artist. Ill. opposite

CRIPPA, Roberto. Italian, born Milan, 1921; lives in Milan
59 *Personage.* 1959. Oil with pasted newspaper and tree bark on wood, 27½x19½″. Collection Mr. and Mrs. E. A. Bergman, Chicago

CROTTI, Jean. French, born Bulle, Switzerland, 1878; died Paris, 1958
*60 *Clown.* 1916. Pasted papers, doll's eyes with black silk lashes, silver wire, on glass, 14⅝x9⅞″. Collection Mme Crotti-Duchamp, Neuilly-sur-Seine. Ill. opposite.

DENNY, Robyn. British, born Surrey, 1930; lives in London
*61 *Collage.* 1957. Oil, torn paper, cloth, canvas, cardboard, 18x21″. Owned by the artist. Ill. p. 106

DIENES, Sari. American, born Debrecen, Hungary, 1899; to U.S.A. 1939; lives in New York
*62 *Construction No. 11.* 1961. Glass bottles, mirror glass, painted wood, cork, aluminum foil, 25½″ high x 11″ wide x 4½″ deep. Owned by the artist. Ill. right

DOMINGUEZ, Oscar. Spanish, born 1905; lives in Paris
*63 *Happy New Year.* (1954). Sheet brass with cut-outs and sardine can keys, 9¼x13¼″, mounted over paper on plywood, 15¾x19¼″. Galleria Schwarz, Milan. Ill. p. 114

DOVE, Arthur G. American, born Canandaigua, New York, 1880; died Centerport, New York, 1946
*64 *Grandmother.* (1925). Shingles, needlepoint, page from the Concordance, pressed flowers, 20x21¼″. The Museum of Modern Art, New York. Gift of Philip L. Goodwin. (NY). Ill. p. 43

65 *Portrait of Alfred Stieglitz.* (1925). Camera lens, photographic plate, clock and watch springs, and steel wool, on cardboard, 15⅞x12⅛″. The Museum of Modern Art, New York. Edward M. M. Warburg Fund. (NY)

*66 *The Critic.* 1925. Cut and pasted newspaper clippings, magazine advertisements, cardboard hat, wool cord, velvet, on cardboard, 19x12½″. The Downtown Gallery, New York. Ill. p. 42

DUBUFFET, Jean. French, born Le Havre, 1901; lives in Paris
67 *The Commander.* 1954. Clinker, 13⅞″ high. Collection Mr. and Mrs. Michael Sonnabend, New York. (NY)

*68 *The Duke.* (1954). Sponge, 24″ high. Stephen Hahn Gallery, New York. Ill. p. 94

69 *The Horseman (Le Reitre).* 1954. Clinker, 14″ high. Collection Mr. and Mrs. Michael Sonnabend, New York. (NY)

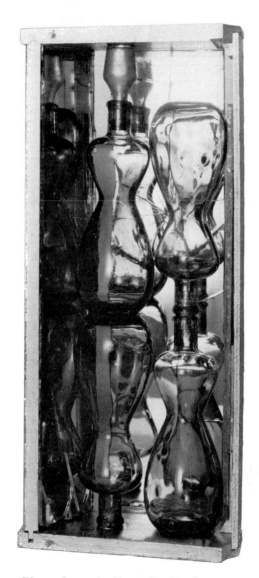

Dienes: *Construction No. 11.* Cat. No. 62

70 *Bread Carrier.* 1955. Ink on paper (*assemblage d'empreintes*), 30x18½".
Collection N. Richard Miller, New York

*71 *Georges Dubuffet in the Garden.* 1956. Cut-up oil paintings on canvas
(*assemblage*), 61x36". Collection Mr. and Mrs. William H. Weintraub, New York. (NY). Ill. p. 95

*72 *Portrait of a Man* (also known as *Portrait aux gazes*). (1957). Butterfly
wings and watercolor on cardboard, 9¾x6¼". Collection Mme Y.
Silvers, Paris. Ill. p. 93

73 *Tapis tabac.* 1959. Tobacco leaves on cardboard, 17½x19¾".
Collection Mr. and Mrs. Samuel M. Kootz, New York

DUCHAMP, Marcel. American, born Blainville (Seine-Maritime),
France, 1887; lives in New York

*74 *Bicycle Wheel.* Readymade (replica of lost original of 1913). Third
version, 1951. 51⅜" high. Sidney Janis Gallery, New York. Ill.
p. 46

*75 *Bottle Dryer.* 1960. Readymade (replica of lost original of 1914).
Galvanized iron, 22¾x12⅝" (at base). Collection Robert Rauschenberg, New York, Ill. (of original) p. 47

*76 *Comb.* 1916. Readymade. Steel comb, 6½x1¼". Philadelphia
Museum of Art. The Louise and Walter Arensberg Collection.
(NY). Ill. p. 47

*77 *With Hidden Noise* (*à bruit secret*). (1916). Readymade. Ball of twine
in brass frame, 5x5x5". Arensberg added a "hidden noise" to this
object. Philadelphia Museum of Art. The Louise and Walter
Arensberg Collection. (NY). Ill. p. 47

78 *Apolinere Enameled.* 1916-17. Readymade. Painted tin advertisement
for Sapolin Enamel, altered and added to by the artist, 9¼x13¼".
Philadelphia Museum of Art. The Louise and Walter Arensberg
Collection. (NY).

*79 *Fountain.* 1917. Readymade. Urinal, 18" high x 15⅛" wide x 12"
deep. Replica in the original size, 1950. Sidney Janis Gallery,
New York. Ill. (of original) p. 47

*80 *Tu m'.* 1918. Oil and graphite on canvas, with bottle-washing
brush, safety pins, nut and bolt, 27½"x10'2¾". Yale University Art
Gallery, New Haven, Collection Société Anonyme. (NY). Ill. p. 45

81 *L.H.O.O.Q.* 1919. Corrected readymade: reproduction of the *Mona
Lisa* to which Duchamp has added a moustache and beard in
pencil, 7½x5". Pierre Matisse Gallery, New York

*82 *Paris Air.* Readymade (replica of original of 1949), 6" high, labeled:
"50 cc Air de Paris replique type 1949 R.S." Philadelphia Museum
of Art. The Louise and Walter Arensberg Collection. (NY). Ill.
(of original) p. 47

*83 *Fresh Widow.* 1920. Miniature French window, wood frame, and
eight panes of glass covered with leather, 30½x17⅝". The Museum
of Modern Art, New York. Katherine S. Dreier Bequest. (NY).
Ill. p. 44

*84 *Why Not Sneeze?* 1921. Readymade. Marble blocks, in the shape of
lump sugar; wood and cuttlebone, in a small bird cage, 4½" high x
8⅝" long x 6⅜" wide. Applied lettering underneath: "Why not
sneeze Rose Sélavy?" Philadelphia Museum of Art. The Louise and
Walter Arensberg Collection. (NY). Ill. p. 47

85 *The Bride Stripped Bare by Her Bachelors, Even* ("*The Green Box*").
1934. 1" high x 13⅛" long x 11⅛" wide. One of 300 numbered
and signed copies of a collection reproducing 93 manuscript notes,

drawings, and paintings (1911-1915). Paris, Editions Rose Sélavy.
Collection Mr. and Mrs. Leonard Brown, Springfield, Mass.

86 *Boîte-en-Valise* (*Box in a Valise*). (1938-1942). Compartmented cardboard box within a leather-covered case, containing miniature
reproductions of Duchamp's works, 4" high x 14¾" wide x 16⅛"
long. No. 9 of a special edition of 20 copies. "Coloriage" original
(1938) inside front cover. The Museum of Modern Art, New York.
James Thrall Soby Fund

DUCHAMP, Suzanne. French, born Blainville (Seine-Maritime), 1889;
lives in Neuilly-sur-Seine, France

87 *Un et Une menacés,* 1916. Inks and gouache on paper, gears, pl mb
bob, silver wire, copper discs, cord, mounted on canvas, 25⅝x
19¾". Owned by the artist

DUFRÊNE, François. French, born Paris, 1930; lives in Paris
88 "*J.*" 1961. Backs of torn posters, 47¼x35½". Galerie J, Paris

DURKEE, Stephan. American, born New York City, 1937; lives in
New York

89 *Sale.* (1960). Weathered wood box with door; paper, photograph,
electric light bulb, wire, hardware, 8⅜" high x 6⅛" wide x 3"
deep. The Allan Stone Gallery, New York

DŽAMONJA, Dušan. Yugoslav, born Strumica, 1928; lives in Zagreb
90 *Metallic Sculpture.* (1959). Welded iron nails and charred wood,
16⅜" high. The Museum of Modern Art, New York. Philip C.
Johnson Fund

ERNST, Max. French, born Brühl, near Cologne, Germany, 1891.
Settled in France, 1922. 1941-1953 in U.S.A. Became American citizen
in 1948. Returned to France, 1953, taking French citizenship in 1958.
Lives in Huismes (Touraine)

91 *The Hat Makes the Man.* (1920). Pasted papers, pencil, ink, watercolor, 14x18". The Museum of Modern Art, New York. Purchase

*92 *The Chinese Nightingale.* (1920). Pasted photographs and half-tones,
4¾x3⅜". Collection Tristan Tzara, Paris. Ill. p. 38

*93 *Loplop Introduces.* 1932. Pasted paper, watercolor, pencil, photograph, 19⅝x25⅜". Collection Mr. and Mrs. E. A. Bergman,
Chicago, Il. p. 66

ESCOBAR, see Marisol

EXQUISITE CORPSES (collaborative drawings)
94 *Cadavre Exquis: Figure,* by André Breton, Max Morise, Jeannette,
Pierre Naville, Benjamin Perét, Yves Tanguy, Max Ernst (?),
(1928?). Collage of pasted papers, 7¾x3½". The Museum of
Modern Art, New York. Purchase

*95 *Cadavre Exquis,* by André Breton, Greta Knutson, Valentine Hugo,
Tristan Tzara. Copy after a lost original of ca. 1933. Ink, 9½x12".
Collection Mr. and Mrs. Morton G. Neumann, Chicago, Ill. p. 40

FERNANDEZ, see Arman

FIÈVRE, Yolande. French, born Paris, 1915; lives in Paris
96 *The Captives.* 1960. Sponge, driftwood, abrasives, sand, silk, 23⅝x
28½". Galerie Daniel Cordier, Paris

*97 *The Guardians.* 1961. Wood compartments, with driftwood, bark, hair, silk, stones, snakeskin, dried snakes, bullets, 35½x15¾″. Galerie Daniel Cordier, Paris. Ill. p. 126

FINE, Perle. American, born Boston, Massachusetts, 1915; lives in Springs, New York and New York City
*98 *Sudden Encounter.* (1961). Pasted papers, watercolor, charcoal, 21¼x27¾″. Graham Gallery, New York. Ill. p. 98

FOLLETT, Jean. American, born St. Paul, Minnesota, 1917; lives in New York
*99 *Untitled.* (1958). Iron and steel hardware, caster, springs, light switch and socket, cooling coils, window-screen, nails; porcelain faucet-knob, mirror, rope and twine, cinders, on wood, 24x30″. Green Gallery, New York. Ill. p. 124

GARCIA, Mario. American; born New York City, 1927; lives in New York
100 *Sailor to Thy Rest.* (1961). Painted wood boards and rope on wood, 27¾x24¼″. Stable Gallery, New York

GETMAN, William. American, born Buffalo, New York, 1916; lives in Southold, New York
*101 *Maria.* (1958). Torn paper posters, hide glue, on masonite, 47¼x 35¼″. Collection Mr. and Mrs. Eddie Albert, Pacific Palisades, California. Ill. p. 107

GOERITZ, Mathias. German, born Danzig, 1915; lives in Mexico City
*102 *Message No. 14.* "*And thy heaven that is over thy head shall be brass, and the earth that is under thee shall be iron.*" Deuteronomy 28:23. 1959. Tin and iron sheeting with peeling paint and plaster, on painted wood, 28¼x22″. Carstairs Gallery, New York. Ill. p. 129

GOODNOUGH, Robert. American, born Cortland, New York, 1917; lives in New York
103 *Collage.* (1951). Torn and pasted papers, 5x7″. Collection Mr. and Mrs. George Wittenborn, Scarsdale, New York
104 *Horse and Rider.* 1961. Cut-up oil paintings, stapled to plywood, 14⅞x14¾″. Tibor de Nagy Gallery, New York

GRIS, Juan (José Gonzalez). Spanish, born Madrid, 1887; to Paris, 1906; died Paris, 1927
*105 *Breakfast.* (1914). Pasted paper, crayon and oil on canvas, 31⅞x 23½″. The Museum of Modern Art, New York. Acquired through the Lillie P. Bliss Bequest. Ill. p. 20

GROSZ, George. American, born Berlin, 1893; to U.S.A. 1932; died on visit to Berlin, 1959
*106 "*Remember Uncle August, the unhappy inventor.*" 1919. Oil on canvas, with charcoal, cut and pasted magazine advertisements, buttons, 19¼x15⅝″. Collection Mr. and Mrs. Bernard J. Reis, New York. Ill. p. 33

HABERLE, John. American, born New Haven, Connecticut, 1856; died New Haven, 1933
*107 *The Changes of Time.* 1888. Oil and gesso on canvas, mounted on masonite, 23¾x19⅜″. Collection Marvin Preston, West Ferndale, Michigan. Ill. p. 12

HAINS, Raymond. French, born Santerieuc, 1926; lives in Paris
*108 "*De Gaulle compte sur vous, aidez-le.*" (1961). Torn paper posters, 47¼x39⅜″. Collection Mr. and Mrs. Robert C. Scull, Great Neck, New York. Ill. p. 109

HALSTEAD, Whitney. American, born Van Wert, Iowa, 1926; lives in Chicago
109 *Personage.* (1952). Broken spoon, forks, knives; bone, rusted metal flakes, plastic wood, on cardboard, mounted on ink-dyed cloth, 16x13⅜″. Owned by the artist

HAUSMANN, Raoul. Austrian, born Vienna, 1886; lives in Limoges, France
*110 *Mechanical Head.* (1918). Wood, metal, leather, cardboard, 12¾″ high. Collection Frau Hannah Höch, Berlin. Ill. p. 36

HERMS, George. American, born Woodland, California, 1935; lives in Larkspur, California
*111 *Poet.* (1960). Wood table-base, stack of pages tied with string, rusted klaxon, wire, 27″ high. Collection Dr. Arthur J. Neumann, Chicago. Ill. p. 133

HIRSCHER, Heinz E. German, born Stuttgart, 1927; lives in Stuttgart
*112 *Straits of Magellan.* 1960. Driftwood, rusted tin sheeting, chicken wire, crushed tin can, broken enamel clock dial, copper sheeting and wire, leather, fabric, paper, 25¼x15″. Owned by the artist. Ill. p. 125

HÖCH, Hannah. German, born Gotha, 1889; lives in Berlin
*113 *Collage.* (1920). Cut and pasted halftone illustrations, 14x11⅞″. Collection Mr. and Mrs. Morton G. Neumann, Chicago. Ill. p. 33

INDIANA, Robert. American, born New Castle, Indiana, 1928; lives in New York
*114 *Moon.* 1960. Gesso on wood beam; iron and wood wheels, 7′ high. David Anderson Gallery, New York. Ill. p. 141

IRWIN, Gwyther. British, born North Cornwall, England, 1931; lives in London
*115 *Collage No. IX.* (1959). Pasted papers on board, 46x34¾″. Collection Mr. and Mrs. Arnold H. Maremont, Chicago, Ill. p. 103

JACOBS, David T. American, born Niagara Falls, 1932; lives in Columbus, Ohio
*116 *Ursula.* (1960). Welded steel and iron machine parts, 19″ high. Barone Gallery, New York. Ill. p. 146

JACOBSEN, Robert. Danish, born Copenhagen, 1912; lives in Montfermeil, near Paris
*117 *Head with Keys.* (1957). Iron, 27″ high. Collection Mr. and Mrs. Arnold H. Maremont, Chicago. Ill. p. 146

JEAN, Marcel. French, born La Charité-sur-Loire, France, 1900; lives in Paris
*118 *Spectre of the Gardenia.* 1936. Plaster, covered with black cloth; zipper eyes; strip of movie film; 10½″ high. Owned by the artist. See bibl. 172. Ill. p. 64

JESS (Collins). American, born Long Beach, California, 1923; lives in San Francisco
*119 *Nadine.* 1955. Cut and pasted magazine illustrations, windowshade pull, tape, cellophane, on board, 17⅝x24½″. Dilexi Gallery, San Francisco. Ill. p. 111

JOHNS, Jasper. American, born Allendale, South Carolina, 1930; lives in New York
120 *Book.* 1957. Encaustic on open book, 9½x12⅞″. Private collection, New York

KALINOWSKI, Horst-Egon. German, born Düsseldorf, 1924; lives in Paris
121 *May Night*. 1961. Collage, gouache, velvet, metal thread, 12⅝x 22″. Galerie Daniel Cordier, Paris

KIENBUSCH, William. American, born New York City, 1914; lives in New York
122 *New England Collage II*. (1947). Cedar shingles, asphalt roofing, tar paper, etc., nailed to painted board, 21⅛x26⅝″. The Museum of Modern Art, New York. Purchase

KIENHOLZ, Edward. American, born Fairfield, Washington, 1927; lives in Los Angeles
*123 *John Doe*. (1959). Two halves of armless male mannequin in child's perambulator, oil paint, wood, metal, plaster, 41″ high x 19″ wide x34″ deep. Ferus Gallery, Los Angeles. Ill. p. 134
*124 *Jane Doe*. (1959). Wooden sewing chest with fur-rimmed drawers containing painted wooden objects, rubber dolls, and sandpaper; side cabinets, one velvet-lined, head and neck of female mannequin, skirt of white bridal dress, oil paint, 42″ high x 27″ wide x 16″ deep. Collection Miss Laura Lee Stearns, Los Angeles. Ill. p. 134

KIERZKOWSKI, Bronislaw. Polish, born Lodz, 1924; lives in Warsaw
125 *Textured Composition Number 91*. 1959. Iron, perforated metal, cement, plastic, 18⅞x18¼″. Collection Mrs. John D. Rockefeller 3rd, New York

de KOONING, Willem. American, born Rotterdam, The Netherlands, 1904; to U.S.A. 1926; lives in New York
*126 *Study for Woman*. (1950). Oil on paper with pasted colored photo-engraving, 14⅝x11⅝″ (sight). Private collection, New York, (NY). Ill. p. 75
127 *Red Eye*. (1955). Torn oil paintings on paper, mounted on mason-ite, 16¼x14¼″. The Allan Stone Gallery, New York

LABLAIS, Michel. French, born Paris 1925; lives in Paris
128 *Negro*. 1958. Torn and pasted photographs, 10⅞x8¼″. Galerie Daniel Cordier, Paris

LANGLAIS, Bernard. American, born Thomaston, Maine, 1922; lives in New York
129 *Wish-Washy I*. (1958-59). Wood, 3¼x7¾″. The Allan Stone Gallery, New York

LATHAM, John. British, born Africa, 1921; lives in London
*130 *Shem*. 1958. Hessian-covered door, with books, envelopes, stainless steel, copper, and other industrial metals; plaster of Paris, poly-vinyl cement; sprayed paint, oil, metallic and fluorescent paint; polyvinyl acetate; 8′4″x4′. Owned by the artist. Ill. p. 123

LAURENS, Henri. French, born Paris, 1885; died Paris, 1954
*131 *Seated Woman*. (1918). Cut and pasted cardboard, with charcoal, 39x26½″. Collection Mr. and Mrs. G. David Thompson, Pittsburgh. Ill. p. 23

LEWITIN, Landès. American, born Cairo, Egypt, of Romanian parentage, 1892; lives in New York
*132 *Innocence in a Labyrinth*. (1940). Collage of colored photoengrav-ings, 8½x17½″. The Museum of Modern Art, New York. Pur-chase. Ill. below.
133 *Shrine*. (1941). Collage of colored photoengravings, 17½x8½″. Rose Fried Gallery, New York

LOCKS, Seymour. American, born Chicago, Illinois, 1919; lives in San Francisco
134 *Claw*. (1959). Wood, copper foil, nails, bottle caps, jewelry, marbles, shells, fishing floats, laminating resin, clear lacquer, 17⅞″ high x 35⅞″ long. David Cole Gallery, Sausalito, California

LOVE, Jim. American, born Amarillo, Texas, 1927; lives in Houston
135 *Figure*. (1959). Soldered iron rods with brush, 16″ high. Staempfli Gallery, New York

Lewitin: *Innocence in a Labyrinth*.
Cat. No. 132

McCAFFREY, Katherine Hynes. American.
136 *House by the Railroad.* (late 19th century). Colored wool yarn, executed on finely perforated cardboard with "scrap pictures" (colored and black and white lithographic reproductions) attached, 20½x27½". Schenectady Museum Association, New York

McFADDEN, Elizabeth. American, born Belmar, New Jersey; lives in New York
137 *Banners of the Sun.* 1955. Collage of fabric and painted metallic-surfaced paper on corrugated cardboard, 18¼x16⅛". The Museum of Modern Art, New York. Purchase

MAGNELLI, Alberto. Italian, born Florence, 1888; lives in Meudon, near Paris
138 *Collage.* 1949. Cardboard, wrapping paper, newsprint, burlap, with conte crayon, 19¾x25¾". Collection Mr. and Mrs. Harry Lewis Winston, Birmingham, Michigan

MAGRITTE, René. Belgian, born Lessines, 1898; lives in Brussels
*139 Painted bottle with carved wood stopper, 12" high. Collection Mr. and Mrs. Joseph R. Shapiro, Oak Park, Illinois. Ill. p. 60

MALEVICH, Kasimir. Russian, born Kiev, 1878; died Leningrad, 1935
*140 *Lady at the Advertising Pillar.* 1914. Oil on canvas, with pasted printed paper, tissue paper, cotton lace, 28x25¼". Stedelijk Museum, Amsterdam. Ill. p. 31

MALLARY, Robert. American, born Toledo, Ohio, 1917; lives in New York
*141 *Jouster.* 1960. Wood, steel, paper, rag, crushed stone and sand, fiberglas, polyester, 8'6¾"x49¾". The Allan Stone Gallery, New York. Ill. p. 140

MANSO, Leo. American, born New York City, 1914; lives in New York
142 *Oracle.* (1961). Collage of colored papers on board, 10½x13½". Grand Central Moderns, New York

MARCA-RELLI, Corrado. American, born Boston, Massachusetts, 1913; lives in New York
*143 *The Snare.* (1956). Oil on cut-up canvas and cloth, 49⅛x52¾". Collection Mr. and Mrs. Arnold H. Maremont, Chicago. Ill. p. 100

MARISOL (Escobar). Venezuelan, born Paris, 1930; to U.S.A. 1950; lives in New York
*144 *From France.* 1960. Wood construction beam with painted and stenciled wood, carved wood hat forms, plaster castings, glass eyes, baby shoe, 54⅜" high x 21¼" wide x 16" deep. Owned by the artist. Ill. p. 135

MASSON, André. French, born Balagny (Oise), 1896; lives in Paris
*145 *Caryatid.* (1939). Tempera, sand, seaweed, seashells, on wood, 13¾x7⅞". Galerie Louise Leiris, Paris. Ill. p. 62

MEO, Salvatore. American, born Philadelphia, 1920; in Europe 1950-60; lives in New York
146 *Speranza.* 1951. Construction of wood, iron, bottle caps, tin, nails, shoe sole, oil paint, 31x31". Charles Egan Gallery, New York
147 *Totem.* 1961. Construction of roof shingles, asbestos, wire net, rope, glass, metal, nails, oil paint, 80x38". Charles Egan Gallery, New York

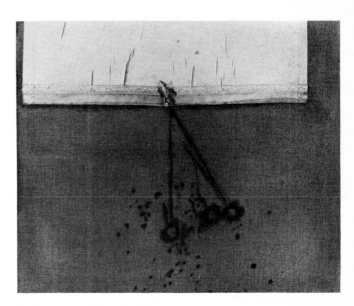

Moskowitz: Untitled. Cat. No. 154

MESENS, E. L. T. Belgian, born Brussels, 1903; has lived in London since 1938
*148 *Mouvement immobile.* 1960. Cut and pasted printed papers, with ink, on cardboard, 13x21½". Grosvenor Gallery, London. Ill. p. 88
149 *Verdure dorées.* 1960. Pasted printed papers, blotting paper, colored tinfoil, thin cardboard, on cardboard, 12⅞x21". Grosvenor Gallery, London

MILLARES, Manolo. Spanish, born Las Palmas, 1926; lives in Madrid
150 *Painting No. 40.* (1959). Oil on cut canvas, stitched with cord, 60x50". Collection Dr. Arthur J. Neumann, Chicago

MIRÓ, Joan. Spanish, born Barcelona, 1893; lives in Mallorca
*151 *Object.* (1932). Painted stone, shell, wood, and mirror-glass on wooden board, 22" long x 9¾" wide. Philadelphia Museum of Art, A. E. Gallatin Collection. Ill. p. 65
*152 *Composition Collage.* 1933. Pasted papers and sandpaper on sandpaper, with gouache, charcoal, pencil and ink, 42½x28". Royal S. Marks, New York. (NY). Ill. p. 62
*153 *Objet poétique.* (1936). Stuffed parrot, stuffed silk stocking with garter and paper shoe, man's hat, cork ball on cord, engraved map, celluloid fish, wood, 33¼" high. Pierre Matisse Gallery, New York. Ill. p. 63

MOSKOWITZ, Robert. American, born Brooklyn, New York, 1935; lives in New York
*154 *Untitled.* 1961. Oil on canvas, with part of a window shade, 24x30". Leo Castelli, New York. Ill. above

MOTHERWELL, Robert. American, born Aberdeen, Washington, 1915; lives in New York
*155 *In Grey with Parasol.* (1947). Oil, pasted papers, imitation leather, on board, 48x36". The New Gallery, New York. Ill. p. 96

*156 *Pyrénéen Collage.* (1961). Oil and pasted papers on paper, 23x30″. Owned by the artist. Ill. p. 97

NESCH, Rolf. Norwegian, born Oberesslingen, Germany, 1893; lives in Aal, Norway
*157 *The Snorer.* (1942-43). Weathered wood boards, carved and burned wood plank, ropes bound with copper wire, corks, brass sheeting, on painted plywood, 30⅝x41½″. Owned by the artist. Ill. p. 115

NEVELSON, Louise. American, born Kiev, Russia, 1900; to U.S.A. 1905; lives in New York
*158 *Royal Tide I.* 1960. Gilded wood, 8′ high x 40″ wide x 8″ deep. Martha Jackson Gallery, New York, Ill. p. 119

NICKLE, Robert. American, born Saginaw, Michigan, 1919; lives in Chicago
*159 *Collage.* (1958-59). Scraps of waste paper, cartons, corrugated cardboard, on board, 20x28½″. Owned by the artist. Ill. p. 98

OPPENHEIM, Méret. Swiss, born Berlin, 1913; lives in Basel and Paris
*160 *Object.* (1936). Fur-covered cup, saucer, and spoon. The Museum of Modern Art, New York. Study Collection. Ill. p. 60
*161 *Squirrel.* (1960). Glass beer mug, with plastic foam and fur on handle, 8⅝″x8½″. Galleria, Schwarz, Milan. Ill. p. 60

OSSORIO, Alfonso. American, born Manila, The Philippines, 1916; lives in East Hampton, New York
*162 *Excelsior.* (1960). Shells, bones, glass eyes, marbles, coins, brass, wood, halftone reproductions, sand, pigment, rope, polyvinyl resin, glue, on wooden board, 56x12″. Betty Parsons Gallery, New York. Ill. p. 105

PAOLOZZI, Eduardo. British, born Edinburgh of Italian parentage, 1924; lives in London
163 *Collage.* 1953. Pasted papers with ink, silk-screen, woodcut, on board, 22x28¾″. Owned by the artist.

PICABIA, Francis. French, born Paris of a French mother and a Cuban father, 1879; died Paris, 1953
*164 *Les Centimètres.* (1918). Oil on canvas, with centimeter tape, paper matches, cardboard match-box covers, 21½x14¾″. Galleria Schwarz, Milan. Ill. p. 32

PICASSO, Pablo. Spanish, born Malaga, 1881; to Paris 1900; lives in Vauvenargues (Bouches-du-Rhône), France
*165 *Bottle of Suze.* (1913). Pasted papers, newsprint, wallpaper, label from bottle of Suze-Apéritif Gentiane, 25¼x19⅝″. Washington University, St. Louis. Frontispiece
*166 *Still Life.* (1914). Painted wood, and upholstery fringe, 10x18⅞″. Collection Roland Penrose, London. Ill. p. 21
*167 *Still Life with a Calling Card.* (1914). Pasted papers and crayon, 5½x8¼″. Collection Mrs. Gilbert W. Chapman, New York. Ill. p. 18

POUSETTE-DART, Richard. American, born St. Paul, Minnesota, 1916; lives in Suffern, New York
168 *The Mirror.* 1948. Oil on pressed stone, with various metals, spoon, bottle caps, safety pin, sardine tin, seashell, buttons, wood, etc., 35x21½″. Betty Parsons Gallery, New York

PRAMPOLINI, Enrico. Italian, born Modena, 1894; died Rome, 1956
169 *Polimaterico automatismo, C.* (1940). Oil on cardboard, with rubber tubing, clock works, mica, sponge, bone, 13x16″. Collection Mr. and Mrs. Harry Lewis Winston, Birmingham, Michigan. (NY)

RAUSCHENBERG, Robert. American, born Port Arthur, Texas, 1925; lives in New York
*170 *Talisman.* (1958). "Combine-painting" of oil paint, paper, fabric, wood, glass, 42x28″. Collection Mr. and Mrs. Arnold H. Maremont, Chicago. Ill. p. 116.
*171 *Canyon.* 1959. "Combine-painting" of oil on canvas on painted wooden boards, pasted printed matter, posters, newsprint, photographs, cloth, metal; stuffed eagle, pillow tied with cord; 6′1″ high x 5′6″ wide x 24¾″ deep. Collection Mr. and Mrs. Michael Sonnabend, New York. Ill. p. 117

RAY, Man. American, born Philadelphia, 1890; lives in Paris
*172 *Theatr.* 1916. Pasted paper, crayon and varnish, on newspaper, mounted on board, 18x24″. Galerie Rive Droite, Paris. Ill. p. 48
*173 *Le Cadeau.* Flat iron with metal tacks, 6½″ high. Collection Mr. and Mrs. Morton G. Neumann, Chicago. Ill. p. 49
174 *Object to be Destroyed.* 1932. Ink drawing, 11½x7¾″. Collection Mr. and Mrs. Morton G. Neumann, Chicago
175 *Optical Hopes and Illusions.* 1944. Banjo with magnifying glass, and painted cork ball on cord, 21¼″ high. Mrs. Pierre Matisse, New York
*176 *Mr. Knife and Miss Fork.* 1944. Knife and fork, wooden beads, net-covered embroidery frame, mounted on cloth, 13⅜x9⅜″. Inscribed "For René Crevel." Galerie Rive Droite, Paris. Ill. p. 86.
*177 *Indestructible Object* (Replica of earlier *Object to be Destroyed*). 1958. Metronome with cutout photograph of eye, on pendulum, 9″ high. Collection Mr. and Mrs. Morton G. Neumann, Chicago. Ill. p. 49
178 *Smoking Device.* 1959. Plastic tubing, marbles, on pipe rack, 7¼′ high x 8¾″ wide. Collection Man Ray, Paris

RAYSSE, Martial. French, born Nice, 1936; lives in Nice
*179 *Nécropole, luxe, et parfum.* 1960. Plastic containers, with cosmetic articles, radio parts, medicinal pills, artificial rose, candies, plastic toys, ping-pong ball, matches, toothbrush, sewing thread, 61¼″ high. Galleria Schwarz, Milan. Ill. opposite

RICHARDS, Ceri. British, born Cardiff, Wales, 1903; lives in London
*180 *The Variable Costerwoman.* 1938. Painted wood, perforated galvanized metal, brass, pearl buttons, rope and string, on partially painted wooden boards, 30¼x29¼″. Owned by the artist. Ill. p. 114

RICHENBURG, Robert. American, born Boston, Massachusetts, 1917; lives in Brooklyn, New York
181 *Paper Collage II.* 1960. Torn and pasted papers on cardboard, 21⅞x27¾″. Tibor de Nagy Gallery, New York

ROTELLA, Mimmo. Italian, born Catanzaro, 1918; lives in Rome
*182 *Before or After.* 1961. Torn and pasted paper posters, mounted on canvas, 59¼x32⅞″. Owned by the artist. Ill. p. 108

RUDOWICZ, Teresa. Polish, born Torun, 1928; lives in Cracow
*183 *Number 51*. 1960. Pasted papers on cardboard, 14x18¼″. Felix
   Landau Gallery, Los Angeles Ill. p. 102

RYAN. Anne. American, born Hoboken, New Jersey, 1889; died New
York, 1954
*184 *Number 48*. (1950). Pasted paper, tinfoil, and cloth on cardboard,
   15¾x12½″. The Museum of Modern Art, New York. Katharine
   Cornell Fund. Ill. p. 99
185 *Collage*. 1953. Pasted paper and cloth, 19x24″. Collection Miss
   Elizabeth McFadden, New York
186 *Collage*. (ca. 1953). Pasted paper and cloth, 12x10¼″. Collection
   Miss Elizabeth McFadden, New York

SAGE, Kay. American, born Albany, New York, 1898; lives in Woodbury, Connecticut
187 *The Great Impossible*. 1961. Painted paper (watercolor and ink),
   cut and pasted on paper, with ground-glass lens and cellulose contact lenses, 12⅝x9″. Catharine Viviano Gallery, New York

de SAINT-PHALLE, Niki. American, born Paris, 1930; lives in Paris
*188 *Tu est moi*. 1960. Steel gear, toy pistol, hunting knife, steel file,
   hammer, cooking fork, nail scissors, razor blade, rope, in plaster,
   on painted plywood, 31½x23⅝″. Private collection, New York.
   Ill. p. 122

SAMARAS, Lucas. American, born Kastoria, Greece, 1936; lives in
West New York, New Jersey
189 Untitled. (1960-61). Plaster over feathers, nails, screws and nuts,
   pins and other hardware, flashlight bulbs, buttons, bullets, mirror-
   glass, toys, aluminum foil, Duco cement, on wood, 23x18½″.
   Green Gallery, New York

SCHLOSS, Edith. American, born Offenbach, Germany, 1919; lives in
New York
*190 *Dow Road*. 1958. Box of weathered wood, with torn printed page
   and wallpaper, lace, glass bottle, sprig of dried cranberry in
   flower, moth, insect, barnacle, 13″ high x 9″ wide x 4½″ deep.
   Owned by the artist. Ill. p. 125

SCHWITTERS, Kurt. German, born Hanover, 1887; died Ambleside,
England, 1948
   The materials used in Schwitters' collages are too diverse to item-
   ize in detail for each work. In general they include tickets, stamps,
   wrappers, labels, newsprint; colored, printed, and plain papers,
   photographs, cardboard, weathered wood and metal, cloth, buttons, wire, etc.
191 *Drawing R 2: Hansi-Schokolade (Zeichnung R 2: Hansi)*. 1918.
   7⅛x5¾″. The Museum of Modern Art, New York. Purchase (NY)
*192 *Drawing 6 (Zeichnung 6)*. 1918. 7x5½″. Collection Mr. and Mrs.
   Solomon Ethe, New York. Ill. p. 52
193 *Picture with Light Center (Bild mit Heller Mitte)*. 1919. 33¼x25⅞″.
   The Museum of Modern Art, New York. Purchase. (NY)
194 *Merz 22*. 1920. 6⅝x5⅜″. The Museum of Modern Art, New York.
   Katherine S. Dreier Bequest

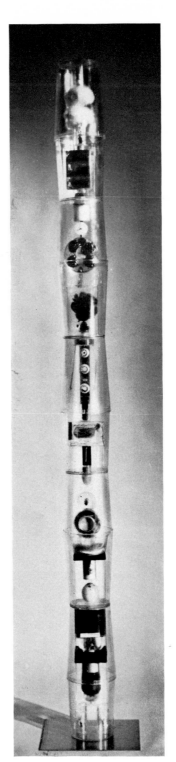

Raysse: *Nécropole, luxe, et parfum.*
Cat. No. 179

195 *Merz 39: Russian Picture* (*Russisches Bild*). 1920. 7⅜x5⅝". The Museum of Modern Art, New York. Katherine S. Dreier Bequest

196 *Merz 83: Drawing F* (*Zeichnung F*). 1920. 5¾x4½". The Museum of Modern Art, New York. Katherine S. Dreier Bequest. (NY)

*197 Untitled. (1920). Oil, pasted papers, etc., on hand mirror, 12½x8⅞". Collection Tristan Tzara, Paris. Ill. p. 57

*198 "*Yes — What?*" ("*Ya — Was Ist?*"). 1920. 41¾x30¼". Collection Mr. and Mrs. James W. Alsdorf, Winnetka, Illinois. Ill. p. 56

199 *Merz 458.* (ca. 1920-22). 7x5⅝". The Museum of Modern Art, New York. Katherine S. Dreier Bequest

200 *Merz 460: Two Underdrawers* (*Twee Onderbroeken*). 1921. 8x6¾". The Museum of Modern Art, New York. Katherine S. Dreier Bequest. (NY)

*201 *Cherry Picture.* 1921. 36⅛x27¾". The Museum of Modern Art, New York. Mr. and Mrs. A. Atwater Kent, Jr. Fund. Ill. p. 53

202 *Large S: Merz 265.* 1921. 8⅛x6⅛". Collection Dr. and Mrs. Hans J. Kleinschmidt, New York

*203 *Merz Construction.* (1921). Painted and carved wood, wire mesh, paper, cardboard, etc., 14½x8½". Philadelphia Museum of Art, A. E. Gallatin Collection. Ill. p. 55

204 *Merz 379: Potsdamer.* 1922. 7⅛x5¾". The Museum of Modern Art, New York. Purchase

205 *Merz: Santa Claus* (*Der Weihnachtsmann*). 1922. 7⅜x6". The Museum of Modern Art, New York. Purchase

206 *Merz 370: Blue Spark* (*Blauer Funken*). 1922. 8⅛x6¾". The Museum of Modern Art, New York. Katherine S. Dreier Bequest. (NY)

207 *Merz 448: Moscow* (*Moskau*). 1922. 6x6¼". The Museum of Modern Art, New York. Katherine S. Dreier Bequest

208 *Merz* [with Emerka Wrapper]. (1922?) 13¾x10⅜". The Museum of Modern Art, New York. Katherine S. Dreier Bequest

209 *The Blue Bird* (*Der Blaue Vogel*). (1922). 8¼x6¾". Collection Mr. and Mrs. Solomon Ethe, New York

210 *Merz 704: Bühlau.* 1923. 5¼x3⅝". The Museum of Modern Art, New York. Katherine S. Dreier Bequest

211 *Merz 2005: Constantinople* (*Konstantinopel*). 1924. 5⅛x4⅛". The Museum of Modern Art, New York. Katherine S. Dreier Bequest

212 *Merz 8.* 1924. 5½x4". The Museum of Modern Art, New York. Katherine S. Dreier Bequest. (NY)

213 *Merz 32.* 1924. 5x3¾". The Museum of Modern Art, New York. Katherine S. Dreier Bequest. (NY)

*214 *Merz Drawing* (*Merzzeichnung*). 1924. 7¾x6⅛". The Museum of Modern Art, New York. Katherine S. Dreier Bequest. Ill. p. 52

215 *Merz:* [with paper lace]. 1925. 4⅜x3⅜". The Museum of Modern Art, New York. Katherine S. Dreier Bequest. (NY)

216 *Merz:* [with black rectangle]. 1925. 5⅝x4½". The Museum of Modern Art, New York. Katherine S. Dreier Bequest. (NY)

217 *Merz 17: Lissitzky.* 1926. 5¼x4⅛". The Museum of Modern Art, New York. Katherine S. Dreier Bequest. (NY)

218 *Merz Drawing E* (*Merzzeichnung E*). 1928. 5¾x4⅛". The Museum of Modern Art, New York. Katherine S. Dreier Bequest. (NY)

219 *Trein.* 1934. 17¾x12½". Collection Mr. and Mrs. Joseph R. Shapiro, Oak Park, Illinois

220 *Merz:* [with a British censor's seal]. (1940-45). 7⅜x6⅛". The Museum of Modern Art, New York. Katherine S. Dreier Bequest. (NY)

*221 *The Neatest Trick of the Month.* (ca. 1943-45). 16¾x21". Collection Richard S Zeisler, New York. Ill. p. 57

222 *Merz Drawing.* 1945. 7⅛x5¾". Collection Mr. and Mrs. George Wittenborn, Scarsdale, New York

223 *S Y Cut.* 1946. 8½x6½". Collection Mr. and Mrs. Harry Lewis Winston, Birmingham, Michigan

224 *Important Wartime Suggestion.* (1947). 19x15". Collection Mr. and Mrs. Morton G. Neumann, Chicago

225 *Merz:* [with the word "Elikan" repeated]. 17⅛x14¼". The Museum of Modern Art, New York. Katherine S. Dreier Bequest. (NY)

SELEY, Jason. American, born Newark, New Jersey, 1919; lives in New York

*226 *Masculine Presence.* (1961). Welded chromium-plated steel automobile bumpers, grill, 7'8" high x 4' wide. Barone Gallery, New York. Ill. p. 147

SEVERINI, Gino. Italian, born Cortona, 1883; lives in Paris and Rome

*227 *Still Life with Cherries.* (1913). Pasted papers, newsprint, with oil, charcoal, and chalk, 20x27". Collection Mr. and Mrs. Harry Lewis Winston, Birmingham, Michigan. Ill. p. 29

SIMON, Sidney. American, born Pittsburgh, 1917; lives in New City, New York

*228 *Kiosk.* (1961). Construction of wood, with maple-wood type, laminated and inlaid into pine boards and ¾" plywood, 37¼" high x 23½" wide x 10⅜" deep. Owned by the artist. Ill. p. 120

SMITH, David. American, born Decatur, Indiana, 1906; lives in Bolton Landing, New York

*229 *Paul's Wood Bob.* (1956). Welded steel rings on steel plate, 10¾x12". Everett Ellin Gallery, Los Angeles. Ill. p. 130

SPOERRI, Daniel. Swiss, born Galati, Romania, 1930; lives in Paris

*230 *Kichka's Breakfast.* 1960. Wooden chair, with tissue-paper-covered wooden board across seat; part of aluminum coffee-maker, china, drinking glass, plastic egg cups with eggshells, cigarette butts, knife, spoons, tin containers for salt, condensed milk, and Nescafe; 14⅜" high x 27¼" wide x 25¼" deep. Galleria Schwarz, Milan. Ill. p. 132

STANKIEWICZ, Richard. American, born Philadelphia, 1922; lives in New York

*231 Untitled. (1961). Welded steel water boiler, sheet steel, oil filters, 67" high x 38" wide. Collection Mr. and Mrs. Burton G. Tremaine, The Miller Company, Meriden, Connecticut. Ill. p. 143

STELLA, Joseph. American, born Muro Lucano, Italy, 1877; to U.S.A. between 1896 and 1900; died New York 1946

232 *Collage No. 6.* (ca. 1921). Pasted papers, 10½x6½". Zabriskie Gallery, New York

*233 *Collage No. 7.* (ca. 1921). Pasted papers and cardboard on paper, 11x8⅞". Zabriskie Gallery, New York. Ill. p. 32

STUART, Ian. Irish, born Dublin, 1926; lives in Glendalough, Eire

234 *Mayo.* (1960). Iron and bone, 21¼" high. The Museum of Modern Art, New York. Purchase

TAJIRI, Shinkichi. American, born Los Angeles of Japanese parentage, 1923; lives in Amsterdam
*235 *Samurai*. (1960). Welded cast iron and forged iron machine parts, ax, nuts and bolts, 33½″ high. Owned by the artist. Ill. p. 146

TANGUY, Yves. French, born Paris, 1900; to U.S.A. 1939; died Connecticut, 1955
*236 *From the other side of the bridge*. (1936). Painted wood and stuffed cloth, 5¼″ high x 18⅝″ long x 8⅜″ wide. Collection Mr. and Mrs. Morton G. Neumann, Chicago, Ill. p. 65

TINGUELY, Jean. Swiss, born Basel, 1925; lives in Paris
237 *Monstranz*. (1960). Iron and steel machine parts, wire, rope, 36″ high. Staempfli Gallery, New York
238 *Makroko*. (1961). Iron and steel machine parts, wire, aluminum, paper, rubber, 19″ high. Staempfli Gallery, New York

TORRES-GARCIA, Joaquin. (1874-1949). Uruguayan, born and died in Montevideo
239 *Relief*. 1931. Painted wood, 30″ high x 7″ wide. Robert Elkon Gallery, New York

TUMARKIN, Yigael. Israeli, born Dresden, Germany, 1933; lives in Tel Aviv and Paris
240 *Rendez-vous in 22984*. 1961. Scrap metal, hardware, printer's type, oil and polyester on canvas, 25⅝x18x3½″. Collection Samuel Dubiner, Tel Aviv

VAIL, Laurence. American, born Paris, 1891; lives in Megève (Haute-Savoie) and Paris
*241 *Bottle*. 1947. Painted bottle, with pasted papers; stopper of cork with glassless spectacles, brush and cloth, 16″ high. Galerie Iris Clert, Paris. Ill. p. 60
*242 *Bottle*. (ca. 1947). Painted bottle and stopper, encrusted with plaster, cork, celluloid, plastic, rubber and tin toys, paper, glass, sponge, feathers, 16¾″ high. Collection Mr. and Mrs. Bernard J. Reis, New York. Ill. p. 60
243 *Composition*. 1951. Container, encrusted with plaster, wood, wire, fishbones, shells, glass, snail-shells, porcelain, chess pieces, nut-shells, dice, pipe bowl, 30″ high. Galerie Iris Clert, Paris

VERLON, André. No citizenship; born at sea (The Mediterranean), 1927; lives in Paris
*244 *No Escape?* (1958). Pasted colored photoengravings on paper, with gouache, 16x11″. Willy Verkauf, Vienna. Ill. p. 110

VICENTE, Esteban. American, born Segovia, Spain, 1906; to U.S.A. 1936; lives in New York
*245 *Collage No. 10*. (1957). Pasted papers, with charcoal, on board, 30x24″. André Emmerich Gallery, New York. Ill. p. 101
246 *Black and Blue*. (1961). Torn and pasted papers, cotton duck, charcoal on canvas, 24x27″. André Emmerich Gallery, New York

de la VILLEGLÉ, Jacques. French; lives in Paris
*247 *6, Bd Poissonnière*. 1957. Torn paper posters, 34⅝x23¼″. Galerie J, Paris. Ill. p. 82

WAGEMAKER, Jaap. Dutch, born Haarlem, 1906; lives in Amsterdam
*248 *Metallic Grey*, 1960. Oil, aluminum egg-slicer and other hardware, wire, plastic, iron, tin, on board, 24x19¾″. Owned by the artist. Ill. p. 122

WARZECHA, Marian. Polish, born Cracow, 1930; lives in Cracow
249 *Number 10*. 1960. Pasted letter papers, with handwriting in ink, on cardboard, with sections embossed; 14x24⅜″. Felix Landau Gallery, Los Angeles

WATTS, Robert. American, born Burlington, Iowa, 1923; lives in Lebanon, New Jersey
250 *Collage*. 1958. Metal foil, cellophane, paper, plastic sheeting, nails, cotton fabric, gauze, on board, 40x28″. Collection Mr. and Mrs. George Brecht, Metuchen, New Jersey

WESTERMANN, H. C. American, born Los Angeles, California, 1922; lives in Chicago
*251 *About a Black Magic Maker*. (1959-60). Slot machine covered with wood-grained linoleum containing miscellaneous objects of plaster, aluminum, fur, rubber, plastic, brass, glass, etc., 83″ high x 26″ wide x 42″ deep. Allan Frumkin Gallery, New York. Ill. p. 85

von WIEGAND, Charmion. American, born Chicago; lives in New York
*252 *Dark Journey*. 1958. Oil on pasted papers, Japanese braided cord, with feather, on cardboard, 19¼x15½″. Owned by the artist. Ill. below

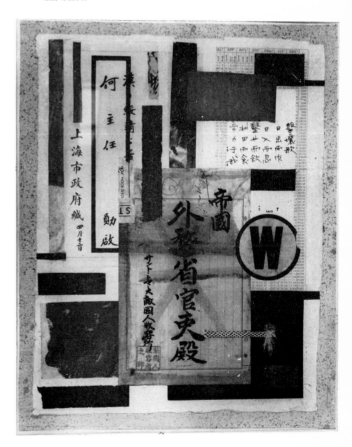

von Wiegand: *Dark Journey*. Cat. No. 252

ASSEMBLAGE: A WORKING BIBLIOGRAPHY

These references make no pretense at providing a comprehensive review of all artists, here and abroad, who may be linked to the concept of assemblage, both yesterday and today. Citations are limited to texts accessible in the Library. Between the polar limitations of time for investigation and space for publication, this bibliography reports selected *titles of general interest* (bibl. 1-40), followed by *articles and reviews* (bibl. 41-108) and some relevant *catalogues of galleries and museums* (bibl. 109-133). A group of miscellaneous citations on *individual artists* (bibl. 134-226) indicates particular attention to Cornell, Duchamp, Man Ray, and Schwitters. Important *bibliographies* in special fields are listed (bibl. 227-232). The preparatory research for *visual* material relevant to assemblage is also listed (bibl. 32). This investigation of widely scattered textual and pictorial resources will be transfered to continuous microfilm and positive paper prints. To this research for image, Lucy Lippard and K. L. McShine have lent their trained academic talents and earned the deep appreciation of this bibliographer. It is expected that educational colorslides of many objects in the show will be provided by Sandak, Inc., the Museum's authorized agency, and black-and-white slides by Taurgo of New York.

BERNARD KARPEL
Librarian of the Museum

GENERAL REFERENCES

1 APOLLINAIRE, GUILLAUME. The Cubist Painters: Aesthetic Meditations, 1913. New York, Wittenborn, Schultz, 1949.
Documents of Modern Art, no. 1, ed. by Robert Motherwell. Bibliography on Apollinaire and cubism by B. Karpel.

2 APOLLINAIRE, GUILLAUME. Calligrammes. Paris, Mercure de France, 1918.
Frequently reprinted.

3 ASPECTS OF MODERN ART. p. 63-81, 101-105 Paris, Lausanne: Bernier; New York, Reynal, 1957.
"Selective Eye, III", selected translations and illustrations from the magazine *L'Oeil*. Includes "The Apollinaire collection" by G. Limbour. — "The international dada" by M. Seuphor. — "André Bréton's collection" by A. Jouffroy.

4 BANHAM, REYNER. Theory and Design in the First Machine Age. p. 106-126 London, Architectural Press; New York, Praeger, 1960.
Chap. 9: Futurism. — Note on futurist typography, p. 111.

5 BARR, ALFRED H., JR. Cubism and Abstract Art. New York, Museum of Modern Art, 1936.
A basic text prepared for an exhibition; illustrations and bibliography.

6 BARR, ALFRED H., JR. Fantastic Art, Dada, Surrealism. Essays by Georges Hugnet, 3 ed. rev. New York, Museum of Modern Art, 1947.
First edition prepared for an exhibition of 1936; bibliography and chronology.

7 BRETON, ANDRÉ. Les Manifestes du Surréalisme [etc.]. Paris, Le Sagitaire, 1955 (c. 1946).

8 COHN, ROBERT G. Mallarmé's Un Coup de Dés: an Exegesis. [New Haven] Yale French Studies Publication, 1949.
Originally a doctoral dissertation. Also enlarged edition: L'Œuvre de Mallarmé: Un Coup de Dés. Paris, Librairie des Lettres, 1951. Includes reduced facsimile of 1914 Mallarmé text.

9 DEMISCH, HEINZ. Vision und Mythos in der Modernen Kunst. Stuttgart, Verlag Freies Geistesleben, 1959.

10 DICTIONNAIRE ABRÉGÉ DU SURRÉALISME. Paris, Galerie Beaux-Arts, 1938.
Definitions, with numerous illustrations. Also insert : Exposition Internationale du Surréalisme, Jan.-Feb. 1938.

11 EHRENZWEIG, ANTON. The Psycho-analysis of Artistic Vision and Hearing. London, Routledge & Kegan Paul, 1953.
"An introduction to a theory of unconscious perception."

12 FRANKENSTEIN, ALFRED. After the Hunt. Berkeley & Los Angeles, University of California Press, 1953.
"William Harnett and other American still life painters, 1870-1900." Also see bibl. 167.

13 FRIEDMAN, B. H., ed. School of New York : Some Younger Artists. New York, Grove; London, Evergreen Books, 1959.
Includes Jasper Johns, Robert Rauschenberg, Richard Stankiewicz and others. Biographical notes.

14 GIEDION-WELCKER, CAROLA. Contemporary Sculpture. 2. ed. rev. New York, Wittenborn, 1961.
Biographies, illustrations; extensive bibliography by B. Karpel.

15 GOLDING, JOHN. Cubism : a History and an Analysis, 1907-1914. p. 103-107 et passim New York, Wittenborn, 1959.
See index references to collage and papier collé, as well as numerous footnotes and citations, e.g. Section d'Or (Paris, Oct. 9, 1911), p. 104, "The first written discussion of collage" by M. Raynal. Bibliography, p. 188-189.

16 GREENBERG, CLEMENT. Art and Culture. Boston, Beacon, 1961.
"Critical essays" including collage, reviews, etc.

17 HAFTMANN, WERNER. Painting in the Twentieth Century. 2 v. New York, Praeger, 1961.
A revision of the original German edition : Vol. I, Text — II, Plates. Both volumes include commentary and illustrations. Numerous biographies and reproductions (including 55 colorplates); deals in book 5 with "the evocative possibilities of the materials" and related forms.

18 HUNTER, SAM. Modern American Painting and Sculpture. New York, Dell, 1959.
Collage, p. 86, 91, 172-173, 183-184. — Cornell, p. 184, pl. 48.

18a JANIS, HARRIET and BLESH, RUDI. Collage. New York, Chilton, 1961.

19 JEAN, MARCEL. The History of Surrealist Painting. With the collaboration of Arpad Mezei. New York, Grove, 1960.
Translated from the French (Paris, Éditions du Seuil, 1959).

20 JONES, BARBARA. Follies and Grottos. London, Constable, 1953.

21 KAPROW, ALLAN. Paintings, Environments, and Happenings [typescript]. [Old Bridge, N. J., July 16, 1960].
Mss. of work in preparation. Extract published in Jackson Gallery

catalogue : New Forms — New Media, Oct. 1960 (bibl. 130), also in "It Is", no. 4, 1959. Photostat on deposit in Museum of Modern Art Library (40 p.). Note bibl. 78.

22 LEVY, JULIEN. Surrealism. New York, Black Sun Press, 1936.
With references to and illustrations by Man Ray and Cornell, including the latter's "Monsieur Phot."

23 LYNCH, JOHN. How to Make Collages. New York, Viking, 1961.
Includes some useful illustrations.

24 MALLARMÉ, STÉPHANE. Un Coup de Dès jamais n'Abolira le Hazard. English translation by Daisy Aldan. [New York] Tiber Press [1956].
"First published in the magazine *Cosmopolis* in 1897 and in book form by Gallimard, a short time later." Text republished 1914. This translation first printed in *Folder 4* (1956).

25 MALEVICH, KASIMIR. The Non-Objective World. Chicago, Theobald, 1959.
Translation of the Bauhaus edition : Die Gegendstandlose Welt (Munich, Langen, 1927).

26 MARINETTI, FILIPPO T. Les Mots en Liberté Futuristes. Milan, Poesia, 1919.
Illustrations include 3 folded plates of futurist typography.

27 MEHRING, WALTER. Berlin Dada. Zurich, Arche, 1959.
"Eine Chronik mit Photos und Dokumenten."

28 MOHOLY-NAGY, LASZLO. Vision in Motion. Chicago, Theobald, 1947.
See index (p. 364) on collage, etc.

29 MON, FRANZ, ed. Movens, Wiesbaden, Limes Verlag, 1960.
Collaborators : W. Höllerer, M. de la Motte. Biographies; chronology of kinetic art. Also French and English summary.

30 MOTHERWELL, ROBERT, ed. The Dada Painters and Poets : an Anthology. New York, Wittenborn, Schultz [1951].
Documents of Modern Art, v. 8. "Did dada die?" — a critical bibliography compiled by Bernard Karpel, p. 318-377.

31 NADEAU, MAURICE. Histoire du Surréalisme. 2 v. Paris, Éditions du Seuil [1945-1948].
Vol. I, text and bibliography. — II, documents. Revised and enlarged edition : Paris, Club des Éditeurs, 1958 (one vol.)

32 NEW YORK. MUSEUM OF MODERN ART. LIBRARY. [Pictorial Research on Images for Assemblage]. New York, 1961.
Pictures of related works of art based on references in the Museum library and photo archive. Material collected largely by Lucy Lippard and K. L. McShine, copied by microfilm and deposited as continuous paper prints in bound format. Also note bibl. 129.

33 POLLACK, PETER. The Picture History of Photography. New York, Abrams, 1958.
"From the earliest beginnings to the present day."

34 PONENTE, NELLO. Modern Painting : Contemporary Trends, p. 163-173 [Switzerland], Skira, 1960.
On artists of the living present, including Burri and Dubuffet. Documentation, p. 185-187.

35 RAYNAL, MAURICE [AND OTHERS]. History of Modern Painting, [Vol. 3] : From Picasso to Surrealism. Geneva, Skira, 1950.
General review and numerous colorplates on modern movements. Comprehensive documentation by Hans Bolliger. Also modified editions (in one vol.) titled "Modern Painting" (1953, 1959).

36 ROSENBLUM, ROBERT. Cubism and Twentieth-Century Art. New York, Abrams, 1961.
Chronology and bibliography.

37 THE SELECTIVE EYE, 1956-1957, p. 96-103. Paris, Lausanne: Bernier; New York : Reynal, 1956.
Includes illustrated article by M. Seuphor : "Futurism . . . yesterday," originally published in *L'Oeil* (Paris).

38 SEUPHOR, MICHEL. The Sculpture of This Century. New York, Braziller, 1960.
Translated from the French (Éditions du Griffon). Biographies and bibliography.

39 SHATTUCK, ROGER. The Banquet Years. New York, Harcourt, Brace, 1958.
Art and artists of Paris in the epoch of Apollinaire. Bibliography.

40 SOBY, JAMES T. Modern Art and the New Past. Norman, University of Oklahoma Press, 1957.
"The importance of collage," p. 82-87, from the *Saturday Review*.

ARTICLES AND REVIEWS

41 ALLOWAY, LAWRENCE. Junk culture. *Architectural Design* 31 no. 3: 122-123 ill. Mar. 1961.

42 ALVARD, JULIEN. Fantaisies typographiques et calligrammes. *Art d'Aujourd'hui* 3 no. 3-4 : 29-32 ill. Feb.-Mar. 1952.
Additional related pictorial material elsewhere in issue.

43 ASHTON, DORE. Plus ça change . . . *Cimaise* 8 no. 52:50-59 ill. Mar.-Apr. 1961.
Multilingual texts.

44 BANHAM, REYNER. Futurism for keeps. *Arts* (*N.Y.*) 35 no. 3 : 33-39 ill. Dec. 1960.

45 BEGG, JOHN. Abstract art and typographic format. *Magazine of Art* 45 no. 1 : 27-33 ill. Jan. 1952.

46 BOULTENHOUSE, CHARLES. Poems in the shape of things. *Art News* 57 no. 7, pt. 2 : 65-83, 178 ill. Nov. 1958.
"1959 Art News Annual XXVIII."

47 BRAQUE, GEORGES. Pensées et réflexions sur la peinture. *Nord-Sud* no. 10 : [2-4] Dec. 1917.
Frequently translated, e.g. in Robert Goldwater and Marco Treves, ed. Artists on Art, New York, Pantheon, 1945 and in Peggy Guggenheim, ed. Art of This Century . . . 1910-1942, New York, 1942.

48 BRETON, ANDRÉ. "C'est à vous de parler, jeune voyant des choses . . ." *XXe Siècle* (n.s.) no. 3 : 27-30 ill. June 1952.
Includes Breton's objects. Also note Jouffroy in bibl. 3.

49 BRETON, ANDRÉ. Equation de l'objet trouvé. *Documents 34* (*Brussels*) (n.s.) no. 1 : 17-24 ill. June 1934.
"Numéro spécial — Intervention surréaliste."

50 BRETON, ANDRÉ. "Rêve-objet." *Cahiers d'Art* 10 no. 5-6 : 125 ill. 1935.

51 BUFFET-PICABIA, GABRIELLE. Matières plastiques. *XXe Siècle* no. 2 : 31-35 ill. May 1, 1938.

52 BUREAU, JACQUES. Morale des mots et des objets. *In* Transfusion du Verbe. p. [10-11] Paris, Éditions de la Main à Plume, 1941.

53 CALAS, NICOLAS. Surrealist intentions. *Trans/formation* (*N.Y.*) no. 1 : 48-52 ill. 1950.

54 CAILLOIS, ROGER. The myth of secret treasures in childhood. *VVV* (*N.Y.*) no. 1 : 4-8 ill. June 1942.

55 CHOAY, FRANÇOISE. Lettre de Paris. *Art International* 4 no. 9 : 34-38 ill. Dec. 1, 1960.
On "sculpteurs américains," "culture de débris"; Arman, Coppel, and others.

56 COLLAGES. *Art d'Aujourd'hui* 5 no. 2-3 : 1-42 ill. Apr. 1954.
Special issue. Texts by Seuphor, Degand, Wescher. Numerous illustrations representative of collage among the modern movements. Also note special number in bibl. 88.

57 COGNIAT, RAYMOND. L'exposition international du surréalisme. *XXe Siècle* no. 1 : 25-28 ill. Mar. 1, 1938.
At the Galerie de Beaux-Arts.

58 CONNOLLY, CYRIL. Surrealism. *Art News* 50 no. 7, pt. 2 : [130]-162, 164, 166, 168, 170 ill. Nov. 1951.
In the Art News Annual 1952.

59 COSNIL, MICHEL-LOUIS. Querelle de formes. *Informations & Documents* (*Paris*) no. 131 : 26-30 ill. Nov. 1, 1960.
Title on cover: Sculptures et assemblages.

60 DEGAND, LÉON. Guillaume Apollinaire et le cubisme. *Art d'Aujourd'hui* 4 no. 3-4 : 71-72 May-June 1953.
Illustrations also p. 70, 73.

61 ESTIENNE, CHARLES. Deux éclairages : Kandinsky & Miró. *XXe Siècle* (n.s.) no. 1 : 21-38 ill. June 1951.

62 GIEDION-WELCKER, CAROLA. Le rétour aux éléments dans la póesie et la peinture. *XXe Siècle* no. 3 : 41-48 ill. June 1952.

63 GINDERTAEL, R. V. Liberté et rigeurs du "collage". *Cimaise* 2 no. 4 : 10-12 ill. Mar. 1955.
Also artists' statements. Illustrated by "exposition de collages à la galerie Arnaud."

64 GOLDWATER, ROBERT. Papiers collés et collages aux États-Unis. *XXe Siècle* no. 8 : 82-83 ill. Jan. 1957.

65 GOOSSEN, E. C. The end of the object. *Art International* 3 no. 8 : 40-42 ill. 1959.

66 GREENBERG, CLEMENT. Art : [a review of the collage show at the Museum of Modern Art]. *The Nation* p. 612-614 Nov. 27, 1948.
"One of the most beautiful shows of modern art ever held in this country."

67 GREENBERG, CLEMENT. The role of nature in modern painting. *Partisan Review* 16 no. 1 : 78-81 Jan. 1949.

68 GREENBERG, CLEMENT. The pasted-paper revolution. *Art News* 57 no. 5 : 46-49, 60-61 ill. Sept. 1958.

69 GUÉGUEN, PIERRE. Esthétique de l'identité : la sculpture (II). *XXe Siècle* no. 2 : 47-48 ill. May 1, 1938.
"Sculpture naturelle et sculpture primitive."

70 GUÉGUEN, PIERRE. Vérités premières de l'espace. *XXe Siècle* (n.s.) no. 2 : 39-42 ill. Jan. 1952.

71 GUEST, BARBARA. Notes on collage. *Arts* (*N.Y.*) 30 no. 6 : 50-51 ill. Mar. 1956.
On the occasion of the Rose Fried gallery show (International Collage). Similarly *Art News* Apr. 1956 (F. Porter), *New Yorker* Mar. 3, 1956 (R. M. Coates).

72 HENZE, ANTON. Über das Basteln in der modernen Kunst. *Kunstwerk* 11 no. 7 : 15-36 incl. ill. Jan. 1958.
Text, p. 15-16, 35-36. "Basteln" includes collages, stabiles, mobiles, montages, constructions, sculptures from "objets trouvés", works by Domela, Arp and examples of dada. Followed, p. 37-38, by Schwitters : Merz (from *Ararat*, 2 no. 1, 1921).

73 HESS, THOMAS B. Mixed mediums for a soft revolution. *Art News* 59 no. 4 : 45, 62 ill. Summer 1960.
Review of "New Forms — New Media ' (bibl. 130).

74 HESS, THOMAS B. Paste mixed with paint. *Art News* 47 : 25-27 Oct. 1948.
Survey of collage technique at the Museum of Modern Art.

75 HULTÉN, K. G. Beknopt overzicht van de ontwikkeling der bewegende kunst in de twintigste eeuw. *In* Bewogen, Beweging. Amsterdam, Stedelijk Museum, 1961.
Insert in bibl. 132.

76 JAGUER, EDOUARD. Avatars de l'objet. *Cahiers du Musée de Poche*. no. 3 : 76-77 ill. Dec. 1959.

77 JOHNSON, E. On the role of the object in analytic cubism : Picasso's "Glass of Absinthe." *Oberlin College Bulletin* 13 no. 1 : 11-25, ill. 1955.

78 KAPROW, ALLAN. "Happenings in the New York scene." *Art News* 60 no. 3 : 36-39 ill. May 1961.
Photos by R. E. McElroy.

79 LEGRAND, FRANCINE-CLAIRE. La peinture et la sculpture au défi. *Quadrum* no. 7 : 23-52 incl. ill. 1959.
English summary p. 186-189.

80 MABILLE, PIERRE. Miroirs. *Minotaure* no. 11 : 14-18, 66 ill. 1938.

81 MADDOX, CONROY. The object in surrealism. *London Bulletin* no. 18-20 : 39-43, 45 ill. June 1940.

82 MARTINI, CARLO. Mallarmé - Marinetti - Gide. *Idea* (*Rome*) May 17, 1953.
On origins of futurist typography. Similarly Renato Mucci: Mallarmé publicista. *Civilitá delle Macchina* Nov. 1954. Related discussion in bibl. 4.

83 MEYERE, VICTOR DE. La sorcellerie en Flandre. *Variétés* 2 no. 6 : 391-398 ill. Oct. 15, 1929.
Includes photos of associated objects.

84 MOTHERWELL, ROBERT. Painters' objects. *Partisan Review* 11 no. 1 : 93-97, Winter 1944.

85 L'OBJET. *Cahiers d'Art* no. 1-2 : 3-66 incl. ill. 1936.
Special number, with numerous illustrations and articles by Zervos, Breton, Éluard, Buffet, Cahun, Dali, Jean and Bellmer.

86 OSBORNE, LUCY E. Carmina figurata & the Aldine Theocritus. *Colophon* part 13 : [8 p.] Spring 1930.
On "early shaped verse" and Apollinarian affinities.

87 REICHARDT, JASIA. Expendable art. *Architectural Design* 30 no. 10 : 421-422 ill. Oct. 1960.
On "autodestructive" art (Tinguely, Metzger).

88 LE PAPIER COLLÉ DU CUBISME À NOS JOURS. *XXe Siècle* (n.s.) no. 6 : 3-60 incl. ill. Jan. 1956.
Special number, with numerous illustrations (pt. col.) and articles by Elgar, Delaunay, Wescher, Seuphor, Bryen, de Solier, Courthion, Verdet, Bertelé.

89 PIPER, JOHN. Abstraction on the beach. *XXe Siècle* no. 3 : 41 ill. July 1, 1938.

90 RESTANY, PIERRE. Fruit de la civilisation de l'image: le poème-objet. *Cimaise* 4 no. 3 : 18-23 ill. Jan.-Feb. 1957.

91 RESTANY, PIERRE. Le baptême de l'objet. 8 p. [Paris, May 1961]. Photocopy of unpublished typescript for forthcoming publication.

92 [REVIEWS]. *Art Index* v. 6, Oct. 1944 — current.
   The articles and reviews reported in this H. W. Wilson Co. periodical index are located partly under "collages" and more frequently under galleries or museums. References other than those already listed in this bibliography would include — M. Breuning : Tracing the history of collage [at the Museum of Modern Art] *Art Digest* Oct. 1, 1948. — On all levels : collages and objects [at the Institute of Contemporary Arts] *Art News* Nov. 1954. — J. S.: Twenty-seven collages [at the Area Gallery, N. Y.] *Art News* Mar. 1959, etc. Consult bibl. 129 for further research in the Index.

93 RODITI, EDOUARD. Interview with Hannah Höch. *Arts* (*N.Y.*) 34 no. 3 : 24-29 ill. Dec. 1959.
   On the Berlin dadaist group.

94 ROSENBERG, HAROLD. Aaron Siskind : the camera and action art. *Art News* 58 no. 6 : 22-23, 57 ill. Sept. 1959.

95 RUBIN, WILLIAM. Younger American painters. *Art International* 4 no. 1 : 25-30 ill. 1960.
   On the occasion of exhibitions at the Stable Gallery and the Museum of Modern Art ("16 Americans"). Also illustrations, p. 24, 31.

96 SANDLER, IRVING H. Ash Can revisited, a New York letter. *Art International* 4 no. 8 : 28-30 ill. Oct. 25, 1960.
   On the Martha Jackson Gallery show ("New Forms — New Media") and related American events.

97 SEUPHOR, MICHEL. Histoire sommaire du tableau-poème. *XXe Siècle* (n.s.) no. 3 : 21-25 ill. June 1952.
   Foreword by André Breton.

98 SEUPHOR, MICHEL. Matière à discussion. *XXe Siècle* (n.s.) no. 5 : 9-14 ill. June 1955.

99 SOBY, JAMES T. The importance of collage. *Saturday Review of Literature* 31 no. 45 : 36-37 ill. Nov 6, 1948.
   Review of show at Museum of Modern Art; reprinted in bibl 40.

100 SPECIAL SCULPTURE NUMBER. *Arts* (*New York*) 32 no. 9 June 1958.
   Includes Clement Greenberg ("Sculpture in our time"), Hilton Kramer ("The sculpture of Louise Nevelson"), etc. Numerous illustrations.

101 STEIN, GERTRUDE. Tender buttons : objects — food — rooms. *Transition* no. 14 : 13-55 Fall, 1928.
   Republication of "Tender Buttons" (N.Y., Claire Marie, 1914).

102 STUDIO TALK : [a column]. *Arts* (*N.Y.*) 1956 — current.
   A series conducted by Vincent Longo, e.g. : Collages combined with painting: interview with Clinton Hill (30 : 64-65 Sept. 1956), later by Bernard Chaet : Paper collage and permanency : interview with Irwin Rubin (32 : 62-63 Jan. 1958), etc.

103 TAYLOR, BASIL. Art — anti-art. *The Listener* p. 819-822 ill. Nov. 12, 1959.
   For the Third Programme broadcast. Continued by Charles Mitchell: The ideas of pre-dada, p. 867-869, Nov. 19, 1959.- Reyner Banham : Primitives of a new art, p. 974-976, Dec. 3, 1959.

104 THWAITES, JOHN A. Dada hits West Germany. *Arts* (*N.Y.*) 33 no. 5 : 30-37 ill. Feb. 1959.
   On the occasion of the Dada exhibition at Düsseldorf (Sept.-Oct. 1958) which was circulated in Germany.

105 TZARA, TRISTAN. Le papier collé ou le proverbe en peinture. *Cahiers d'Art* 6 no. 2 : 61-74 ill. 1931.

106 WATT, ALEXANDER. Paris letter: Nouveaux réalistes. *Art in America* 49 no. 2 : 106-108, 110, 112 ill. 1961.

107 WESCHER, HERTA. Les collages cubistes. *Art d'Aujourd'hui* 4 no. 3-4 : 33, 42 May-June 1953.
   Intervening pages consist of relevant illustrations.

108 WESCHER, HERTA. Collages and the breakdown of optical unity. *Graphis* 11 no. 57 : 52-59 ill. 1955.
   Trilingual text.

SELECTED CATALOGUES

109 PIERRE, GALERIE. Picasso : Papier Collés, 1912-1914. Paris, Feb. 20-Mar. 20, 1935.
   Introduction by Tristan Tzara.

110 GOEMANS, GALERIE. Exposition de Collages. Paris, Mar. 1930.
   Essay by Aragon : La peinture au défi. 32 p., 23 ill.

111 NEW YORK. MUSEUM OF MODERN ART. Cubism and Abstract Art. New York, Mar. 2-Apr. 19, 1936.
   386 works shown. See bibl. 5.

112 NEW YORK. MUSEUM OF MODERN ART. Fantastic Art, Dada, Surrealism. New York, Dec. 7, 1936-Jan. 17, 1937.
   694 works shown. See bibl. 6.

113 LONDON GALLERY. Surrealist Objects & Poems. London, 1937.
   Foreword by H. Read; brief poems by Read, Mesens, Gascoyne, etc. List of 138 exhibits; [20] p., 8 ill.

114 TAKIGUCHI, SHUZO AND YAMANAKA, TIROUX, ed. Album Surréaliste. Tokyo, June 1937.
   Special issue of the magazine *Mizué* for an international exhibition held at the Nippon Salon. Exhibited works, selected by the artists, consisted of 80 watercolors, sketches and prints, 350 photos and objects. Index and bibliography in French; 112 p. including numerous illustrations.

115 GUGGENHEIM, PEGGY, ed. Art of This Century . . . 1910 to 1942. New York, "Art of This Century," 1942.
   Preface by André Breton on the genesis of surrealism; also other texts and notes. Laurence Vail, p. 123. 156 p. with numerous illustrations including objects and collages.

116 NEW YORK. MUSEUM OF MODERN ART. Collage. New York, Sept. 21-Dec. 5, 1948.
   No catalogue issued, only publicity release and checklist of 102 works. Library has photo album of show which was organized by Margaret Miller. For reviews see bibl. 66, 74, 92, 99.

117 CALIFORNIA PALACE OF THE LEGION OF HONOR. Time and Man. San Francisco, Mar. 29-May 11, 1952.
   "An idea illustrated by an exhibition," including objects. Text by S. Peterson: Lub dub vs ticktack.

118 SAMLAREN, GALERIE. Objekt eller Artefakter. Verkligheten för Verklig. [Stockholm], Feb.-Mar. 1954.
   Catalogue and exhibit by K. G. Hultén and O. Reutersvärd. Over 41 items on display; [12] p. incl. ill.

119 LONDON. INSTITUTE OF CONTEMPORARY ART. Collages and Objects. London, Oct. 13-Nov. 20, 1954.
83 exhibits listed. Reviewed in *Art News*, p. 54, Nov. 1954.

120 FRIED, ROSE, GALLERY. International Collage Exhibition. New York, Feb. 13-Mar. 17, 1956.
For reviews see bibl. 71.

121 FEIGL, MARIE-SUZANNE, GALERIE. Collages, 1912-1956. Basel, Galerie d'Art Moderne, Dec. 8, 1956-Jan. 15, 1957.
Quotes from Knaurs Lexikon "Moderne Kunst"; 4 p., ill.

122 ALAN GALLERY. Beyond Painting. New York, Dec. 29, 1958-Jan. 24, 1959.
Preface, 11 works.

123 HOUSTON. CONTEMPORARY ARTS MUSEUM. The Disquieting Muse: Surrealism. Houston, Jan. 9-Feb. 16, 1958.
Text by J. Levy, J. MacAgy, H. Read; 48 p. incl. ill.

124 HOUSTON. CONTEMPORARY ARTS MUSEUM. Collage International: From Picasso to the Present. Houston, Feb. 27-Apr. 6, 1958.
Introduction by J. MacAgy; 30 p. incl. ill.

125 ARTS CLUB OF CHICAGO. Art and the Found Object. Chicago, June 1959.
A checklist of "colorslides by Whitney Halstead."

126 HOUSTON. CONTEMPORARY ARTS ASSOCIATION. Out of the Ordinary. Houston, Nov. 26-Dec. 27, 1959.
Preface by Harold Rosenberg; n.p., ill.

127 NEW YORK. MUSEUM OF MODERN ART. Sixteen Americans, ed. by Dorothy C. Miller. New York, Dec. 16, 1959-Feb. 14, 1960.
"Statements by the artists and others." Included Johns, Nevelson, Rauschenberg, Stankiewicz, etc.; 96 p. incl. ill.

128 CORDIER, DANIEL, GALERIE. Exposition Internationale du Surréalisme, 1959-1960. Paris, (opened) Dec. 15, 1959.
On cover: Boite alerte — Missives lascives. Directed by A. Breton, M. Duchamp, etc.; 146 p. incl. ill.

129 NEW YORK. MUSEUM OF MODERN ART. LIBRARY. [Scrapbook of Catalogues, Clippings and Pictures on Collage and the Object, Constructions, et cetera]. New York, 1960- date.
A compilation including some of the items noted above, as well as 21 photos of mannequins exhibited in the London surrealist show (1936) and related items. Typical documents include: *Collage* (Newark Museum, Apr. 28-June 12, 1960). — *But . . . Is It Art?* (Renaissance Society of Chicago, Oct. 17-Nov. 12, 1960). — *Le Relief* (Galerie XXe Siècle, Dec. 2-31, 1960), etc. Also note bibl. 32.

130 JACKSON, MARTHA, GALLERY. New Forms — New Media I. New York, Oct. 1960.
Foreword by M. Jackson; essay by L. Alloway: Junk culture as a tradition; Allan Kaprow: Some observations on contemporary art. 22 p., ill., 75 exhibits. Reviewed adversely in *Arts* (Nov. 1960, p. 50) by H. Kramer. Also see bibl. 73, 96.

131 SCHWARZ, GALLERIA. L'Oggetto nella Pittura. Milan, Mar. 1-15, 1961.
Part of an experimental series, continuing as: Daniel Spoerri (Mar. 16, 1961). — Gruppo Phases (May 1961), etc.

132 AMSTERDAM. STEDELIJK MUSEUM. Bewogen, Beweging. Amsterdam, Mar. 10-Apr. 17, 1961.
In association with the Modern Museum, Stockholm. Catalogue edited by K. G. Hultén (and others) who contributes an extensive introduction (13 p.). Oblong format, 32 p., incl. ill., with folded insert.

133 JACKSON, MARTHA, GALLERY. Environments, Situations, Spaces. New York, May 25-June 23, 1961.
Statements by Brecht, Dine, Gaudnek, Kaprow, Oldenburg. 10 leaves, no ill.

INDIVIDUAL ARTISTS

Supplemental citations will be found in the general references above, e.g. bibl. 100, 127, etc.

Bellmer

134 BELLMER, HANS. Poupée. *Minotaure* no. 6 : 30-31 18 ill. Winter 1935.
"Variations sur le montage d'une mineure articulée."

135 BELLMER, HANS. Les Jeux de la Poupée. Illustrés de Textes par Paul Éluard. Paris. Les Éditions Premières, 1949.
15 mounted color photographs. Also GLM edition (Paris, 1936).

Burri

136 SWEENEY, JAMES J. Burri. [9] p. plus 20 pl. (pt. col.) Rome, L'Obelisco, 1955.
Bibliography. Also Sweeney foreword for catalogue: Paintings of Alberto Burri (Arts Club of Chicago, 1958).

César

137 COOPER, DOUGLAS. César. 39 p. plus 24 pl. Amriswill, Bodensee, 1960.
Biographical and bibliographical notes.

138 HANOVER GALLERY. César : Recent Sculpture. [36] p. incl. ill. London, Oct. 6-Nov. 18, 1960.
Introduction by P. Restany; biographical notes, exhibitions, collections. Complemented by: SAIDENBERG GALLERY. César: Sculpture 1952-1961. [36] p. incl. ill. New York, Apr. 7-May 6, 1961. Similar documentation; introduction by Sam Hunter.

139 RESTANY, PIERRE. César le ferrailleur. *Art International* 3 no. 5-6 : 68-70 ill. 1959.

Colla

140 ALLOWAY, LAWRENCE. Ettore Colla : Iron Sculpture. [80] p. incl. ill. Rome, Grafica, 1960.
Text (10 p.) in English and Italian. Statement by Colla.

141 LONDON. INSTITUTE OF CONTEMPORARY ART. Colla. [12] p. ill. London, Aug.-Sept. 1959.
Texts by L. Alloway and C. Fox Delloye.

Cooper

142 GIMPEL FILS. Austin Cooper. [8] p. ill. London, May 1961.
Preface by H. Read; list of 27 works.

Coppel

143 SEUPHOR, MICHEL. J. Coppel : préface en trois tempe. *I 4 Soli* 3 no. 5 : 8 ill. Sept.-Oct. 1956.

Cornell

144 CORNELL, JOSEPH. The crystal cage : [portrait of Berenice]. *View* 2 no. 4 : 10-16 ill. Jan. 1943.
Also cover, and illustrations, p. 21-24.

145 CORNELL, JOSEPH. "Enchanted wanderer" : excerpt from a journey album for Hedy Lamarr. *View* 1 no. 9-10 : 3 port. Dec. 1941-Jan. 1942.
> Also see special number of *View* : Max Ernst (2 no. 1, Apr. 1942).

146 CORNELL, JOSEPH. Monsieur Phot. p. 77-88 *In* Julien Levy, Surrealism. New York, Black Sun Press, 1936.
> Other references and illustrations : p. 28, 77-88, 182-183. Includes "Objects by Joseph Cornell" exhibited Nov. 26-Dec. 30, 1932 : "minutiae, glass bells, shadow boxes, coups d'oeil, jouets surréalistes."

147 EGAN GALLERY. Aviary by Joseph Cornell. 3 p. New York, Dec. 1949.
> 26 exhibits, with preface by D. Windham. Reviewed by Belle Krasne. *Art Digest* 25 no. 6 : 17, Dec. 15, 1950.

148 GOOSSEN, E. C. The plastic poetry of Joseph Cornell. *Art International* 3 no. 10 : 37:40 ill. 1959-1960.

149 GRIFFIN, HOWARD. Auriga, Andromeda, Cameoleopardalis. *Art News* 56 no. 8 : 24-27, 63-65 ill. Dec. 1957.
> On Cornell.

150 HUGO GALLERY. Romantic Museum. . . 4 p. ill. New York, Dec. 1946.
> "Constructions and arrangements by Joseph Cornell."

151 T[YLER], P[ARKER]. [Joseph Cornell at the Stable Gallery]. *Art News* 56 no. 9 : 18-19 Jan. 1958.

Crippa

152 JOUFFROY, ALAIN. Manifeste pour Crippa. *Art International* 5 no. 3 : 26-31 ill. Apr. 5, 1961.

Dali

153 DALI, SALVADOR. Apparitions aérodynamiques des "êtres-objets." *Minotaure* no. 6 : 33-34 ill. Winter 1935.

154 HALSMAN, PHILIPPE. The Dali cat episode. *Photography Workshop* (Chicago) 1 no. 2 : 38-39 ill. Fall 1950.

Dominguez

155 HUGNET, GEORGES. L'objet utile, à propos d' Oscar Dominguez. *Cahiers d' Art* 10 no. 5-6 : 139 ill. 1935.

Duchamp

156 DUCHAMP, MARCEL. Marchand du Sel : Écrits de Marcel Duchamp. 213 p. ill. Paris. Le Terrain Vague, 1958.
> "Réunis et présentés par Michel Sanouillet. Bibliographie de Poupard-Lieussou."

157 LEBEL, ROBERT. Marcel Duchamp. 191 p. ill. New York, Grove, 1959.
> Extensive documentation and illustration.

158 RUBIN, WILLIAM. Reflexions on Marcel Duchamp. *Art International* 4 no. 9 : 49-53 ill. Dec. 1, 1960.

159 VIEW MAGAZINE. Marcel Duchamp Number. 56 p. ill. New York, 1945.
> Series 5, no. 1, Mar. 1945. Essays and reproductions.

160 ZURICH. KUNSTGEWERBEMUSEUM. Dokumentation über Marcel Duchamp. 40 p. ill. Zurich, June 30-Aug. 28, 1960.
> Texts by H. Fischli, M. Bill, S. Stauffer, M. Duchamp.

Ernst

161 CREVEL, RENÉ. Mr. Knife, Miss Fork. Translated by Kay Boyle. Paris, Black Sun Press, 1931.
> Illustrated with 19 original photograms by Max Ernst.

162 LIEBERMAN, WILLIAM S., ed. Max Ernst. 63 p. ill. New York, Museum of Modern Art, 1961.
> Exhibition catalogue, with chronology and bibliography.

Evans

163 KIRSTEIN, LINCOLN. Walker Evans : American Photographs. 198 p. incl. 37 plates. New York, Museum of Modern Art, 1938.

Goeritz

164 RIGG, MARGARET. Messages : the sculpture paintings of Mathias Goeritz. *Motive* (Nashville, Tenn.) 20 no. 5 : 16-28 ill. Feb. 1960.
> Reproductions from work exhibited at the Carstairs Gallery, N. Y.

Haberle

165 FRANKENSTEIN, ALFRED. Haberle : or the illusion of the real. *Magazine of Art* 41 no. 6 : 222-227 ill. Oct. 1948.

Harnett

166 BORN, WOLFGANG. William M. Harnett : bachelor artist. *Magazine of Art* 39 no. 6 : 248-254 ill. Oct. 1946.
> Extract from his work on "American Still Life Painting" (1947).

167 FRANKENSTEIN, ALFRED. New Harnett discoveries. *Magazine of Art* 44 no. 2 : 62-66 ill. Feb. 1951.
> See also bibl. 12.

Heartfield

168 HEARTFIELD, JOHN. John Heartfield : Photomontagen zur Zeitgeschichte. 101 p. incl. ill. Zurich, Kultur und Volk, 1945.
> Articles by A. Drurus, W. Reiss, L. Aragon (1934-1935). References also in bibl. 30.

Hugnet

169 HUGNET, GEORGES. La Septième Face du Dé : Poëmes—Découpages. 24 p. plus 20 plates. Paris, Bucher, 1936.

Jacobsen

170 IONESCO, EUGÈNE. Jacobsen's dolls. *XXe Siècle* (n.s.) no. 15 : 111-115 ill. Christmas 1960.

171 LOUISIANA MUSEUM. Robert Jacobsen. 28 p. ill. Louisiana (Humlebaek), Oct. 10-Nov. 15, 1959.
> Texts by E. Ionesco and W. Schwartz (reprints in Danish); list of 111 works.

Jean

172 JEAN, MARCEL. A phantom's genealogy. 3 p. 1961.
> Typescript on "The Spectre of the Gardenia," with references.

Johns

173 ROSENBLUM, ROBERT. Jasper Johns. *Art International* 4 no. 7 : 74-77 ill. Sept. 25, 1960.

Lebrun

174 LANGSNER, JULES. Rico Lebrun. *Arts & Architecture* 74 no. 6 : 21, 31 June 1957.

Mesens

175 PERRE, HUGO VAN DE. Interview E. L. T. Mesens. 5 leaves, London, Feb. 1961.

"Opname : 13 februari 1961 voor Belgische Radio & TV."

176 GROSVENOR GALLERY. Mesens. [14] p. ill. London, Feb. 8-28, 1961.

With list of exhibited works and biographical note.

Motherwell

177 ASHTON, DORE. Art: [Robert Motherwell]. *Arts & Architecture* 74 no. 7 : 4 ill. July 1957.

On Janis Gallery show of paintings and collages. Also note bibl. 30, 84.

Nesch

178 HENTZEN, ALFRED. Rolf Nesch : Graphik, Materialbilder, Plastik. [122] p. ill. Stuttgart, Belser, 1960.

Nevelson

179 ARP, JEAN. Louise Nevelson. *XXe Siècle* (n.s.) no. 14 : [101] ill. June 1960.

In supplementary "chroniques du jour."

180 ASHTON, DORE. Louise Nevelson. *Cimaise* 7 no. 48 : 26-36 ill. Apr.-June 1960.

Quadrilingual text.

181 ROBERTS, COLETTE. L' "ailleurs" de Louise Nevelson. *Cahiers du Musée de Poche* no. 4 : 77-83 ill. May 1960.

Oppenheim

182 SCHWARZ, GALLERIA. Meret Oppenheim. [11] p. ill. Milan, Nov. 16-30, 1960.

With list of exhibited works; 11 reproductions.

183 THOLLANDER, LEIF. Meret Oppenheim. *Konstrevy* 36 no. 2 : 76-77 ill. 1960.

Ray

184 RAY, MAN. Alphabet for Adults. 40 leaves (illustrated). Beverly Hills, Copley Galleries, 1948.

185 RAY, MAN. Champs Délicieux. Album de Photographies avec une Préface de Tristan Tzara. Paris [Société Générale d'Imprimerie et d' Édition], 1922.

Edition of 40 albums with 12 original photos and rayograms. Copy 41 with "les épreuves des cliches rayés."

186 RAY, MAN. Facile. Poèmes de Paul Éluard, Photographies de Man Ray. 14 p. incl. plates. Paris, G. L. M., 1935.

Also limited editions.

187 RAY, MAN. Les Mains Libres. Dessins illustrés par les Poèmes. [206] p. incl. plates Paris, Bucher, 1937.

188 RAY, MAN. Photographs by Man Ray, Paris 1920-1934. [104] p. incl. ill. Hartford, Conn., J. T. Soby, 1934.

Texts by Ray, Éluard, Breton, Sélavy (Duchamp), Tzara.

189 RAY, MAN. Sur le réalisme photographique. *Cahiers d' Art* 10 no. 5-6 : 120-121 ill. 1935.

190 RAY, MAN. To Be Continued Unnoticed. [14] p. ill. Beverly Hills, Copley Galleries, 1948.

"Some papers by Man Ray in connection with his exposition, December 1948." Only 275 copies issued loose in folio (125 copies with autographed photo).

191 ALLOWAY, LAWRENCE. Some London exhibitions : man made objects. *Art International* 3 no. 5-6 : 61 1959.

192 KLEIN, FRED. Man Ray for Art : [a publicity release]. 8 leaves Paris, June 4, 1954.

Biographical data and memoirs on the occasion of his retrospective at the Galerie Furstenberg.

193 LONDON. INSTITUTE OF CONTEMPORARY ARTS. Works of Man Ray. 16 p. ill. London, Mar. 31-Apr. 25, 1959.

With text by the artist. Retrospective includes 61 exhibits (rayographs, drawings, books, photograhs).

194 WALDBERG, PATRICK. Bonjour monsier Man Ray. *Quadrum* no. 7 : 91-102 ill. 1959.

Rauschenberg

195 ASHTON, DORE. Art : derivation of dada . . . *New York Times* p. 42 Mar. 1, 1960.

Review of Rauschenberg's constructions and collages at the Castelli gallery.

196 METRO (Milan) no. 2:30 — 61 ill. 1961.

Essays by Gillo Dorfles, John Cage and Dore Ashton on Rauschenberg. Also partial Italian texts.

197 PARINAUD, ANDRÉ. Un "misfit" de la peinture New-Yorkaise se confesse. *Arts (Paris)* no. 821:18 May 10-16, 1961.

An interview with Rauschenberg.

Rodia

198 GUÉGUEN, PIERRE. Architecture et sculpture naives. *Aujourd'hui* 2 no. 8 : 38-41 ill. June 1956.

Of associated interest as "le palais du facteur Cheval à Hauterives," followed by Silby below.

199 SILVY, MAURICE. Les tours de Watts, de Sam Rodillo à Los Angeles. *Aujourd'hui* 2 no. 8 : 42-45 ill. June 1956.

200 [SIMON RODIA'S TOWERS]. 4 p. ill. Los Angeles, Committee for Simon Rodia's Towers in Watts, n.d.

Copy in library has insert: a bibliography of 17 references "to May 1, 1959."

201 THE WATTS TOWERS. [20] p. ill. Los Angeles, Committee for Simon Rodia's Towers, 1961.

Refers to color film (written by William Hale, narrated by Jeff Corey) and color-slide program by Seymour Rosen.

Schwitters

202 SCHWITTERS, KURT. Die Blume Anna. Berlin, Der Sturm [1922].

"Elementar . . . eine Gedichtsammlung aus dem Jahren 1918-1922."

203 SCHWITTERS, KURT. Konsequente Dichtung. *G (Berlin)* no. 3 : 45-47 ill. June 1924.

204 SCHWITTERS, KURT. Merz. *Der Ararat* 2 : 3-11 ill. 1921.

Text, p. 3-9; poems, p. 9-11; ill. p. 17, 19. Often published in whole or part.

205 SCHWITTERS, KURT, ed. Merz. No. 1-24. Hannover, 1923-1934.

Last number titled "Ursonate." For details and other bibliography on Schwitters see R. Motherwell-B. Karpel (bibl. 30).

206 SCHWITTERS, KURT. . . . Revolution in Revon. *Transition* no. 8 : 61-76 Nov. 1927.

207 SCHWITTERS, KURT. Sensation. *i 10* (Amsterdam) 1 no. 7 : 270-271 1927.
> Additional texts in no. 8-9 : 312-316 ("Anregung einer Systemschrift"). — no. 11 : 392-402 ("Meine Sonate in Urlauten : Zeichenerklärung").

208 SCHWITTERS, KURT. Stil oder Gestaltung. *L'Esprit Nouveau* (Paris) no. 1 : [48-49] [Apr. 1927].
> Also: Plastische Schreibung [p. 46], in the only issue of this magazine (edited by Michel Seuphor).

209 SCHWITTERS, KURT. Sturm Bilderbuch IV : Kurt Schwitters. 32 p. incl. ill. Berlin, Der Sturm [1920].
> Introduction by Otto Nebel (p. 1-2).

210 BERGGRUEN & CIE. Kurt Schwitters : Collages. [28] p. ill. Paris, Berggruen, [1954].
> Collection Berggruen no. 7. Texts by Schwitters, C. Bryen; chronology by H. Bolliger.

211 GIEDION-WELCKER, CAROLA. Schwitters, or the allusions of the imagination. *Magazine of Art* 41 no. 6 : 218-211 ill. Oct. 1948.

212 KESTNER GESELLSCHAFT. Kurt Schwitters. [50] p. ill. Hannover, 1956.
> Exhibition catalogue, Feb. 4-Mar. 11, lists 208 works. Text by W. Schmalenbach; chronology by H. Bolliger.

213 LORD'S GALLERY. Kurt Schwitters, 1887-1948. 32 p. ill. London, 1958.
> Exhibition catalogue, Oct.-Nov., lists 117 exhibits. Preface by A. Bowness also published in Schwitters catalogue (1959) by the Arts Council. Reviews: *Art News* 57 no. 6 : 43 Oct. 1958 (by J. Rusell). — *Art News and Review* 10 no. 19 : 5-7 Oct. 11, 1958 (by E. L. T. Mesens).

214 SCHMALENBACH, WERNER. Kurt Schwitters. *Werk* 43 no. 5 : 153-158 ill. May 1956.
> Followed, p. 159, by Hans Bolliger : Lebensdaten von Kurt Schwitters. Supplemental essay by Schmalenbach in *Art International* 4 no. 7 : 58-62 ill. Sept. 25, 1960.

215 SCHWITTERS, ERNST. Kurt Schwitters: "An Anna Blume" . . . "Die Sonate in Urlauten" . . . Long playing record, 33⅓ rpm. [London, Lord's Gallery, 1958].
> With introduction by the son to his reading of the father's poems.

216 THEMERSON, STEFAN. Kurt Schwitters in England. 62 p. ill. London, Gaberbocchus Press, 1958.
> Includes typography, manuscript and documentary reproductions.

217 VAHLBRUCH, HEINZ. Kurt Schwitters, Maler und Dichter. *Kunstwerk* 7 no. 3-4 : 27-30 1953.
> Includes "Merzmanifest."

218 VORDEMBERGE-GILDEWART, F. Kurt Schwitters (1887-1948). *Forum* (Amsterdam) no. 12 : 356-362 ill. 1948.

Tinguely

219 KLUVER, J. W. The garden party. 13 p. [1960].
> Photostat of typescript (by an associate) on Tinguely's "destructive construction no. 1" at the Museum of Modern Art, Mar. 17, 1960.

220 REUTERSVÄRD, OSCAR. Jean Tinguely. *Konstrevy* 35 no. 5-6 : 192-201 ill. 1960.

221 STAEMPFLI GALLERY. Jean Tinguely : Recent Constructions. 20 p. ill. New York, 1961.
> Catalogue, Apr. 4-22, listing 27 works; miscellaneous texts and chronology.

222 WAALS, J. C. VAN. Dada rediviva. *Museumjournal* (Otterloo) 6 no. 9-10 : 198-202 ill. Apr.-May 1961.

Verlon

223 HOFMANN, WERNER. Verlon. [12] p. plus 42 ill. Paris, Vienna : Verkauf [1960].
> Trilingual text.

Wagemaker

224 EINDHOVEN. STEDELIJK VAN ABBE MUSEUM. Jaap Wagemaker — Theo Wolvecamp — Jean Stekelenburg — Jef Diederen. Eindhoven, 1960.
> Exhibited Feb. 25-Mar. 20; shown at Arnhem Mar. 30-Apr. 30. List of works, chronology, statement by the artist.

225 GRAHAM GALLERY. 3 Artists from Thingdom, Holland : Lucebert, Mooy, Wagemaker. New York, 1960.
> Shown Apr. 5-30, with introduction and documentation by Jan Vrijman; prefatory note by W. Sandberg for "Your Thingdom." Printed at Hilversum, Netherlands.

Westermann

226 FRUMKIN, ALLAN, GALLERY. H. C. Westermann : Recent Works. [16] p. ill. Chicago, 1958.
> Essay by Dennis Adrian; biographical note.

BIBLIOGRAPHIES

227 BOLLIGER, HANS. [Bibliographies] *In* HISTORY OF MODERN PAINTING. 3 v. Geneva, Skira, 1949-1950.
> Supplemented by his documentation in "Dada" ed. by Willy Verkauf, p. 176-183. New York, Wittenborn [1957].

228 EDWARDS, HUGH. Surrealism and Its Affinities : The Mary Reynolds Collection, a Bibliography. 131 p. ill. Chicago, Art Institute of Chicago, 1956.

229 GAFFÉ, RENÉ, COLLECTION. Bibliothèque de M. René Gaffé . . . Auteurs du Mouvement Dada et du Groupe Surréaliste . . . 88 p. ill. Paris, [Hotel Drouot], 1956.
> Sales catalogue, Apr. 26-27, with preface by Georges Blaizot.

230 KARPEL, BERNARD. Did Dada Die? a Critical Bibliography. *In* The Dada Painters and Poets, ed. by Robert Motherwell. p. 318-377 ill. New York, Wittenborn, Schultz, 1951.

231 MATARASSO, H., LIBRARIE. Surréalisme : Poésie et Art Contemporains . . . 108 p. ill. Paris, 1949.
> "Catalogue à prix marqués : autographes, dessins, revues, manifestes, éditions originales, libres illustrés, ouvrages sur l'art d'aujourd'hui."

232 NICAISE, LIBRAIRIE. Cubisme, Futurisme, Dada, Surréalisme : Catalogue no. 10. 272 p. ill. Paris, 1960.
> A dealer's collection, exhibited Nov. 25-Dec. 20, reported in an outstanding illustrated catalogue of literature, éditions-de-luxe and documents.

INDEX

Figures in italic indicate illustrations

abstract expressionism, 32, 74, 84, 87, 89
accidentalism, see chance
affiches lacérées, see lacerated posters
Alloway, Lawrence, 73, 123, 149
anti-art, 10, 34, 82, 87, 90, 132; see also dada, futurism
Apollinaire, Guillaume, 10, 12, 13, *14*-15, 16, 17, 21, 25, 26, 39, 74, 85, 121, 151 n.24, 212; see also calligrams
Arman (Fernandez), 84, 86, 108, *127*
Arp, Jean, *35, 37*, 39, 81
assemblage, 3-dimensional, 10, 24, 25, 26, 32, 38, 39, 41, 45, 50, 72, 73, 76, 78, 79, 81-92, 93, 118, 150 n.5, 151 n.23; see also collage, literature and assemblage, music and assemblage
automatism, 13, 17, 39, 41, 48
automobile, 26, 85, 87-88, 89, 144

Baader, Johannes, *34*
Baargeld, J. T. (Alfred Grünewald), *38*
Baj, Enrico, 86, *104, 113*
Baldaccini, see César
Balla, Giacomo, 26
Banham, Reyner, 87
Barr, Alfred H., Jr., 10, 40, 150 n.5
Baudelaire, Charles, 10, 37
Baxter, John, *141*
Beckett, Samuel, 87
Bergson, Henri, 83-84
Beynon, Eric, *142*
Boccioni, Umberto, 25, 26, *28*, *30*, 85, 87
Bontecou, Lee, *139*
books and newspapers in assemblage, 46, 74, 85, 86, 116, 123, *133*
Bouras, Harry, 84, *121*
Braque, Georges, 10, 15, 17, *18*, *19*, 22, 23, 24, 25, 26, 93, 150 n.5, 152 n.6
Brauner, Victor, *64*, 81
Brecht, George, *155*
Breton, André, 14, 17, 39, *40*, *67*
Bryen, Camille, *61*
Burri, Alberto, 81, *136*, *137*

Cage, John, 17, *116*
Calder, Alexander, 89
calligrams, *14*, 15
Cangiullo, Francesco, 26
Caravaggio, Michelangelo, 22
Carrà, Carlo, 26, *27*

Cendrars, Blaise, 13, 15
César (Baldaccini), 88, *144*, *145*
Cézanne, Paul, 9, 11-12, 13, 21
Chamberlain, John, 85, 88, *138*
chance, 13, 17, 35, 37, 39, 40, 45, 46, 82, 83, 85; see also automatism
Chardin, Jean-Baptiste, 9
Chessman, Caryl, 89
Chirico, Giorgio de, 40, 74
city, influence of, 38, 73-74, 76, 88
Cocteau, Jean, 17
Coetzee, Christo, *131*
Cohen, George, 86, *112*
Colla, Ettore, *148*, *149*
collage, 10, 14, 15, 17, 22, 25, 26, 34, 39, 40, 41, 73, 74, 76, 87, 93, 97, *136*, 150 n.5; see also assemblage, literature and assemblage, music and assemblage, *papier collé*, prototypes, typography
Collins, see Jess
combine-paintings, see Rauschenberg
Conner, Bruce, 74, 86, *89*, *128*
constructions, 23, 39, 46, 89
constructivism, 25, 89
Cooper, Austin, *102*, 150 n.5
Copley, William, 88
Cornell, Joseph, *68-71*, 72, 73, 85, 86
Corsi, Carlo, *156*
Courbet, Gustave, 88
Crivelli, Carlo, 26
Crotti, Jean, *156*
cubism, 9, 10, 13, 14, 15, 16, 17, *21-25*, 26, 30, 37, 40, 72, 73, *136*, 150 n.5
cummings, e. e., 17

dada, 11, 13, 14, 16, 17, 25, 30, 32-39, 40, 41, 76, 87, 93, 136, 149, 150 n.5
dada objects, 34, 149
Dali, Salvador, 39, *58*, 59
Debussy, Claude, 13
décollage, 23, 76, 150 n.5; see also lacerated posters
découpage, 150 n.5
de Kooning, Willem, 32, 74, *75*, 87, 150 n.5
Delaunay, Robert, 12, 14, 24, 26
Denny, Robyn, *106*
Dienes, Sari, *157*
Dine, James, 88, *91*
Dominguez, Oscar, *114*
Dove, Arthur G., *42*, *43*
Dreier, Katherine, 45
Dubuffet, Jean, 84, *93-95*, 150 n.5

Duchamp, Marcel, 10, 14, 17, 23, 32, 37, 39, *44-47*, 72, 73, 76, 83, 86, 87, 88, 89, 123, 149
Duchamp, Suzanne, 46
Duhamel, Georges, 15

Eisenstein, Sergei, 150 n.5, 151 n.23
Eliot, T.S., 17, 81
empreintes, see Dubuffet
environment, 72ff, 81, 82, 87
environments, see happenings
Ernst, Max, *38*, 40-*41*, *66*
Escobar, see Marisol
expressionism, 26, 39
exquisite corpse, *40*, 41

Fantin-Latour, Henri, 9
Fernandez, see Arman
Fièvre, Yolande, *126*
film, 13, 14, 39, 92, 150 n.5, 151 n.23
Fine, Perle, *98*
Flannagan, John, 85
Follett, Jean. *124*
found objects, 15, 46, 73, 81, 83, 84, 85, 118, 149
free words, *16*, 25, 26
frottage, 41
Fry, Roger, 11, 13
futurism, 12, 13, 14, 15, 16, 25, 30, 32, 33, 37, 39, 73, 74, 87

Gabo, Naum, 89
Gaudì, Antoni, 78
Géricault, J.L.A. Théodore, 136
Gestalt psychology, 12, 150 n.11
Getman, William, *107*
Gide, André, 13, 17, 25, 88, 92
Goeritz, Mathias, *129*
Gonzalez, Julio, 149
Gorky, Arshile, 39
Goya y Lucientes, Francisco de, 10
graffiti, 76, 84
Gris, Juan, 17, *20*, 22-23, 24, 81, 86, 151 n.37
Grosz, George, *33*
Guys, Constantin, 10, 37

Haberle, John, *12*, 150 n.5
Hains, Raymond, 82, *109*
Hamilton, Richard, 88
happenings, 88, 90-*91*, 92
Harnett, William, 9
Hausmann, Raoul, *36*, 50
Herms, George, 81, *133*
Hiroshima, 89

Hirscher, Heinz E., *125*
Höch, Hannah, *33*
Huelsenbeck, Richard, 32, 33, 151 n.52
Hugnet, Georges, 40
Hugo, Valentine, *40*

ideograms, 15
illusionism, 22, 45, 81, 82; see also *trompe l'oeil*
impermanence and assemblage, 46, 85, 89, 90, 92, 93
impressionism, 11, 12, 13, 22, 26, 39
Indiana, Robert, *141*
Ingres, Jean-Auguste Dominique, 10, 87
Ionesco, Eugene, 17, 87
Irwin, Gwyther, *103*, 150 n.5

Jacob, Max, 13, 15
Jacobs, David, *146*
Jacobsen, Robert, *146*
Jarry, Alfred, 37, 87
Jean, Marcel, 39-40, *64*
Jess (Collins), *111*
Johns, Jasper, 74
Jouffroy, Alain, 82, 132
Joyce, James, 17
junk culture, 15, 32, 73, 76, 78, 85, 88, 89, 136, 143, 145
juxtaposition, 9, 10, 13, 15, 17, 25, 26, 38, 39, 40, 41, 45, 74, 81, 83-84, 87, 88, 151 n.23

Kafka, Franz, 87
Kahnweiler, Daniel-Henry, 21, 22, 23
Kandinsky, Wassily, 24
Kaprow, Allen, 85, 88, 90-91
Kienholz, Edward, 81, 85, 86, *134*
Kinetic art, see movement
Knutson, Greta, *40*
Kupka, Frank, 24

lacerated posters, 23, 76, 82; see also *décollage*
Latham, John, 86, *123*
Laurens, Henri, *23*
Lautréamont, Compte de (Isadore Ducasse), 39, 40, 151 n.63
Lebenstein, Jan, 84
Leiris, Michel, 22
letters and numbers in art, 9, 10, 22, 84, 85, 87, 121, 123; see also typography
Lewitin, Landès, *160*
Lissitzky, El, 24
literature and assemblage, 13, *14*, 15-17, 22, 25, 37, 50, 86, 92, 143

McShine, K. L., 68-70
Magritte, René, 39, 41, *60*

Malevich, Kasimir, 24, *31*
Mallarmé, Stéphane, 13, 39, 123
Mallary, Robert, *140*
Mancini, Antonio, 26
Manet, Edouard, 9, *10-11*, 37
Marca-Relli, Corrado, *100*
Marin, John, 74
Marinetti, Filippo Tommaso, 15, *16*-17, 25, 26, 37, 74
Marisol (Escobar), *135*
Masson, André, 39, *62*
materials, 14, 22, 23, 25-26, 38, 39, 45, 48, 50, 68, 72, 73, 77, 78, 81, 83, 84, 86, 88, 89, 90, 92, 94, 118, 123, 136, 143, 145, 149, 150 n.5; see also catalogue of exhibition, 153-165
Matisse, Henri, 11, 150 n.5
Matta Echaurren, Roberto, 39
media, see materials, techniques
Mercure de France, 16
Merz, see Schwitters
Mesens, E.L.T., *88*
Metzger, Gustave, 89
Mildew manifesto against rationalism in architecture, 76
Miller, Henry, 76
Miró, Joan, 25, 39, *62*, *63*, *65*, 72, 73
Moholy-Nagy, Laszlo, 89
Mondrian, Piet, 12, 21, 24, 30, 74, 81, 87
Monet, Claude, 11, 12, 76
Moore, Marianne, 17
Moskowitz, Robert, *161*
Motherwell, Robert, 72, *96-97*
movement, 26, 89, 91
Mumford, Lewis, 76
Muñoz, Lucio, 84
music and assemblage, 17, 22, 25, 39
musique concrète, 17

neo-dada, 32, 38-39, 87, 145
Nesch, Rolf, *115*
Nevelson, Louise, 72, 118, *119*
new realists, 82-83, 145, 150 n.5
newspapers in assemblage, see books . . .
New York, 74, 76, 91, 92
Nickle, Robert W., *98*
non-art, 34, 82, 85, 132; see also found objects, readymades
numbers in art, see letters and numbers . . .

object-picture, 25, 81
object sculpture, 26
objects, 9, 10, 13, 21, 22, 25, 26, 48-49, 68-70, 73, 81, 82, 83, 84-85, 86, 87, 89, 90, 92, 123, 132; see also dada objects, found objects, object sculpture, readymades, surrealist objects

objets trouvés, see found objects
Oldenburg, Claes, 91
Oppenheim, Merét, *60*
Ossorio, Alfonso, *105*

Paalen, Wolfgang, *58*
papier collé, 10, 14, 15, 23, 72, 85, 97, 150 n.5
perishable media, see impermanence
photomontage, 34, 150 n.5
Picabia, Francis, *32*, 149
Picasso, Pablo, *frontispieec*, 8, 9, *10*, 15, 17, *18*, *21*, 22, 23, *24*, 25, 26, 73, 74, 81, 85, 86, 87-88, 93, 150 n.4, 150 n.5
poetry and assemblage, see literature and assemblage
Pollock, Jackson, 39, 87
Porter, Fairfield, 143
Pound, Ezra, 17
Poussin, Nicolas, 11, 22
prototypes, assemblage and collage, 10, *11*, *12*, *13*, 72, 73, 83, 150 n.5

Rauschenberg, Robert, 23, 25, 72, 74, 89, *116*, *117*
Ray, Man, *48-49*, 73, *86*
Raysse, Martial, *163*
readymades, 23, 34, *46*, 47, 76, 83
Redon, Odilon, 136
Rembrandt van Rijn, 46, 136
Renoir, Pierre Auguste, 136
Restany, Pierre, 82, 108, 145
Reverdy, Pierre, 13
Ribemont-Dessaignes, Georges, 35
Richards, Ceri, *114*
Rimbaud, Arthur, 10, 39
Rivers, Larry, 88
Rodia, Simon, 72-73, *77-80*
Rotella, Mimmo, 82, *108*
Rousseau, Henri, 40
Rudowicz, Teresa, *102*
Rubens, Peter-Paul, 118, 136
Ryan, Anne, 85, *99*

Saint-Phalle, Niki de, *122*
Salmon, André, 15
Sartre, Jean-Paul, 87
Satie, Erik, 10, 17
Schloss, Edith, 125
Schwitters, Kurt, 25, 39, *50-57*, 72, 73, 76, 85, 87, 118, 136, 143
Seley, Jason, 88, *147*
Seligmann, Kurt, *59*
Seurat, Georges, 12, 78
Severini, Gino, 26, *29*
Shattuck, Roger, 13

Simon, Sidney, *120*
simultanéisme, see Delaunay
Smith, David, *130*, 149
snare pictures, see Spoerri
Soby, James Thrall, 40
Soirées de Paris, 15, 151 n.24
Spoerri, Daniel, *9*, 82, 83, *132*
Stankiewicz, Richard, 88, 89, *143*
Steinberg, Saul, 17
Steinitz, Kate, 50
Stella, Joseph, *32*
Stevens, Wallace, 143
surrealism, 13, 14, 16, 17, 39-41, 83, 87, 88, 136
surrealist objects, 41, 59, 72, 83, 86
Sweeney, James Johnson, 136
symbolism, 13, 14
Sypher, Wylie, 17

tableau-objet, see object-picture
Tajiri, Shinkichi, *146*

Tanguy, Yves, *65*
Tapiès, Antoni, 84
Tatlin, Vladmir, 23
Taeuber-Arp, Sophie, 150 n.5
Taylor, Basil, 90
technique, 74, 85, 87, 89, 93, 97; see also materials
Tinguely, Jean, 85, 89, *90*, 108
trompe-l'oeil, 9, 21, 81; see also illusionism
Tumarkin, Yigael, 84
typography, 16-17, 26, 39, 50, 81, 85; see also letters and numbers in art
Tzara, Tristan, 35, 39, 40, 151 n.52

urban influences, see city, influence of
Utamaro, 10

Vaché, Jacques, 87
Vail, Laurence, *60*
Varèse, Edgar, 17

Velazquez, Diego, 10
Verlon, André, *110*
Vicente, Esteban, *101*
Villeglé, Jacques de la, *82*

Wagemaker, Jaap, 84, *122*
Watts Towers, Los Angeles, see Rodia
Webern, Anton von, 17
Westermann, H. C., *85*
Whistler, James Abbott McNeill, 10
Whitehead, Alfred North, 12
Whitman, Robert, 85
Wiegand, Charmion von, *165*
words and assemblage, see literature and assemblage, typography
Wright, Frank Lloyd, 76

Zen Buddhism, 37, 89
Zola, Emil, 10, 11